True Stories about Washington's Heroes, Villains & Belles

Capital Tales

by MAXINE ATWATER

```
Library of Congress Cataloging-in-Publication Data

Atwater, Maxine H.
    Capital tales : true stories about Washington's heroes, villains &
  belles / by Maxine Atwater.
       p.    cm.
    Includes bibliographical references (p.    ) and index.
    ISBN 1-880774-21-6
    1. Washington (D.C.)--Biography--Anecdotes.  2. Washington (D.C.)-
  -History--Anecdotes.  3. Washington (D.C.)--Guidebooks.  I. Title.
  F193.A88  1995
  920.0753--dc20
    [B]                                                        95-39418
                                                                   CIP
```

CAPITAL TALES; TRUE STORIES ABOUT WASHINGTON'S HEROES, VILLAINS & BELLES.

Copyright (c) Maxine Atwater 1996

All rights reserved. No part of this book may be reproduced or transmitted in any form or by any means, electronic or mechanical including but not limited to photocopying, recording or by any information storage or retrieval system without written permission from the author, except for the inclusion of brief quotations in a review.

Library of Congress No. 95-39418

ISBN 1-880774-21-6

Published by
  Mercury Press
  PO Box 34933
  Bethesda, MD 20827-0933
  301 279-7093

Dedication

To my husband, Roger,
whose love and support
made this book possible

About the Author

Maxine Atwater is founder and president of Special Interest Tours Inc., which specializes in unusual tours of the Washington D.C. area. She often guides the tours she organizes for convention groups, for her commentary drawing on her extensive knowledge of the capital. To add a new dimension to her tours, Atwater exercises her story-telling skills. Whether telling a brief anecdote between sightseeing stops or a longer story when traveling across town, she brings the Washington scene dramatically to life.

A writer for more than forty years, over one hundred of her travel articles have been published in leading newspapers and magazines. Her previous books include:

Washington Revealed, 1992, John Wiley & Sons, New York

New Emerging Careers For Today, Tomorrow and in the 21st Century, 1989, Garrett Park Press, Maryland

Rollin' On: A Wheelchair Guide to U.S. Cities, 1978, Dodd, Mead & Co., New York

The Natural Food Cookbook, 1974, Nitty Gritty, Productions, San Francisco

A native of San Francisco, she came to Washington in 1976. Since that time, when not conducting book research at the Library of Congress, she has covered most of the capital by foot or by bicycle. With the excitement known to any explorer, she has sought out the Washington that hides behind, above, below and beyond the obvious. With **Capital Tales** she extends her love of exploration to uncovering dramatic moments in the lives of those whose spirits linger -- only slightly beyond our perception -- at the sites and on the streets of the Washington we know today.

Preface

Many people, who participate in the tours I conduct in Washington, D.C., ask me why there isn't a book of stories about the people associated with the famous sites?

I've heard their question to mean that, after a hard day of sightseeing, they really yearn to curl up with a book that expands on their sightseeing experiences. Most aren't looking for more facts. Instead they want to know the people who lived in the museum houses and worked in the grand public buildings they've seen on their tours of the capital. They yearn to know these heroes, villains and belles of yesterday and thus to feel the human and emotional scale of history.

Now, **Capital Tales** brings the past to life. For only through the telling of stories can we connect so effectively with those who came before us.

In telling seventeen stories and ten vignettes, **Capital Tales** focuses on dramatic episodes lived by Washington's history-makers. The stories go beyond mere biographies; instead they spotlight a specific moment -- a turning point -- that occurred in the capital city.

Most of the stories in **Capital Tales** open as the main character faces a turning point, often a crisis. As many of the dramas unfold, readers move back through time so they can see how the character got into the situation he or she faces. After this flash-back, the story picks up where it left off to reveal the resolution.

The people who take the center stage of each chapter do so because they lived a story worth telling. Simply being famous wasn't enough.

To find their stories, I scoured the biographies and autobiographies of over a hundred candidates. I used as my criteria for selection that individuals lived a portion of their lives in Washington and that the spotlighted story unfolded here. I selected both heroes and villains, and the famous and the forgotten. The collective lives told here span over 150 years from 1791 to the 1940s. Stories are arranged in chronological order.

Many of the leading actors and actresses in these dramas will be familiar to readers. Others who passed across the stage that is Washington have faded from view. Since social and political climates change -- particularly in Washington with shifts in presidential administrations -- celebrities come and go. The super-star of one day fades away almost overnight. Particularly during Civil War years, many were pushed to the wings who otherwise would have garnered enduring fame,

Since the world simply doesn't remember everyone worth recalling, **Capital Tales** brings some of the most interesting back into focus.

By doing so, the book helps readers discover more of their American heritage. And, as we meet or renew our acquaintance with some of our country's most important and colorful people, we also discover the common bonds that unite us in the past -- and bring us together in the present.

My thanks and appreciation to those who helped in the research and writing of Capital Tales: advisor Roger Ellman, editor Libby Dudley, copy editor June Haley, librarian Matthew Gilmore, historian William C. Dickenson, Smithsonian Associates's Senior Program Coordinator Karen M. Gray, Red Cross historian Patrick Gilbo, author Michael W. Kauffman, author Pamela Scott, designer William Duffy, publisher Robert Calvert Jr.

Maxine Atwater, Washington, D.C.
1996

Contents

Pierre Charles L'Enfant
    Genius, Pauper, Immortal   1
    Pierre Charles L'Enfant's Washington   8

Dolly Madison
    Fleeing Amidst Flames   11
    Dolly Madison's Washington   18

Stephen Decatur
    Gun Shots at Bloody Run   21
    Stephen Decatur's Washington   26

Anne Royall
    She Faced a Ducking-Stool Death Ride   28
    Anne Royall's Washington   35

Peggy Eaton
    She Caused A President To Dismiss His Cabinet   37
    Peggy Eaton's Washington   46

Mary & Emily Edmonson
    Escape to Freedom   48
    Mary & Emily Edmonson's Washington   60

Daniel Webster
    He Spoke And Sang From His Heart   63
    Daniel Webster's Washington   69

Mary Custis Lee
    Roses & Tombstones   71
    Mary Custis Lee's Washington   80

Belle Boyd
    The Siren Spy   82
    Belle Boyd's Washington   93

Frederick Douglass
    Triumph at the White House   95
    Frederick Douglass' Washington   103

Daniel Sickles
    He Got Away With Murder   105
    Daniel Sickles' Washington   112

John Wilkes Booth
    The Actor's Final Role   115
    John Wilkes Booth's Washington   123

Clara Barton
    Greatest American Woman   125
    Clara Barton's Washington   135

Henry Adams
    Number Two of Hearts   137
    Henry Adam's Washington   144

John Philip Sousa
    He Played To Their Hearts   147
    John Phillip Sousa's Washington   153

Evalyn Walsh McLean
    The Diamond's Curse   155
    Evalyn Walsh McLean's Washington   162

Alice Roosevelt Longworth
    Outrageous Alice   165
    Alice Roosevelt Longworth's Washington   174

More Capital Tales   175

    Diplomat Baron Alexander de Bondisco   175

    Artist Constantino Brumidi   176

    Bootlegger George C. Cassiday   177

    Banker William W. Corcoran   177

    Industrialist Henry Clay Folger   178

    Aviation Pioneer Samuel Perpont Langley   179

    Publisher Eleanor (Cissy) Patterson   179

Portrait Painter Rembrandt Peale   179
Adventurer Albert Pike   180
President Woodrow Wilson   181

Illustration Credits   183

Bibliography & Notes   185

Index   200

Illustrations

Pierre Charles L'Enfant
    Portrait   0 (opposite p1)
    L'Enfant Tomb   8

Dolly Madison
    Portrait   10
    Dolly's Lafayette Square Residence   18

Stephen Decatur
    Portrait   20
    Decatur House   26

Anne Royall
    (No likeness is known to exist.)
    Old City Hall   35

Peggy Eaton
    Portrait   36
    Andrew Jackson Statue   46

Emily & Mary Edmonson
    Portrait   54
    Fort Washington   60

Daniel Webster
    Portrait   62
    Webster statue   69

Mary Custis Lee
    Portrait   70
    Arlington House   80

Belle Boyd
    Portrait   83
    U.S. Capitol Dome   93

Frederick Douglass
    Portrait   94
    Cedar Hill Home   103

Daniel Sickles
    Portrait   105
    St. John's Church   112

John Wilkes Booth
    Portrait   115
    Ford's Theatre   123

Clara Barton
    Portrait   124
    Glen Echo Home   135

Henry Adams
    Portrait   136
    Saint Gauden's Memorial to Clover Adams   144

John Philip Sousa
    Portrait   146
    Commandant's House, Marine Barracks   153

Evalyn Walsh McLean
    Portrait   155
    Embassy Row Residence   162

Alice Roosevelt
    Portrait   164

Pierre Charles L'Enfant

1754-1825

Genius, Pauper, Immortal

Engineer and designer L'Enfant remains today America's most notable city planner. His breadth of vision in laying out the America's capital city, resulted in a spaciousness that remains unmatched in the United States.

Born in Paris, the talented Frenchman came to America in 1777 as a commissioned lieutenant of engineers. During his duty at Valley Forge, *he met* George Washington *who later chose the young officer to survey the site and create the plan for the new federal city.*

When L'Enfant came to Washington, D.C., in 1791, his head filled with grand visions, he began a struggle that ended in triumph. Almost a century after he died in disgrace and poverty, fame finally came to L'Enfant.

"The roof is already down with part of the brickwork," Pierre Charles L'Enfant reported in describing his demolition of the house of Daniel Carroll of Duddington. "The whole will ... be leveled to the ground before the week is over."[1]

After tearing down the house of the nephew of the federal city commissioner, L'Enfant explained his reason: "It was necessary," he said. "I proceeded ... with as much confidence as in directing a tree to be cut down or a rock to be removed ...."[2]

Commissioned by George Washington to design the capital city, L'Enfant laid out the city on a grand scale -- "proportional to the greatness" of America's capital itself. To create the wide vistas L'Enfant drew diagonal avenues as lines of communication to connect principal buildings. If anything obstructed one of these avenues, the symmetry he sought would be ruined. Since preserving balance and unity was crucial to the realization of the masterpiece he envisioned, L'Enfant would fight any attempt to alter his plan.

Thus, when the Carroll house obstructed one of L'Enfant's diagonal avenues, L'Enfant acted; he had to protect the integrity of his plan. He also feared that the private interests of leading citizens like Carroll would supersede those of the nation -- unless he interceded.

* * * * * *

The impassioned L'Enfant, Paris native and artist's son, had joined the French colonial troops and come to America in 1777 to help fight the British. "A tall, erect man, fully six feet in height, finely proportioned, nose prominent, of military bearing, courtly air and polite manners ... [he] would attract attention in any assembly."[3]

At Valley Forge, L'Enfant served as aide to Baron von Steuben, executing the drawings for a training manual that the Prussian general (who didn't speak English) used to drill the raw Yankee recruits for warfare. In quiet moments, L'Enfant drew pencil portraits of his fellow officers. Because of his skill, he came to the attention of George Washington who, to fulfill the request of his ally the Marquis de Lafayette, needed a portrait of himself; L'Enfant drew Washington.

Pierre Charles L'Enfant

From that introduction, L'Enfant's relationship with Washington grew. At the end of the war, L'Enfant volunteered to handle some business in Paris for the Society of the Cincinnati, of which Washington was president. L'Enfant had designed a medal for this society of revolutionary war officers. On this trip to see his father, L'Enfant was to deliver letters to Lafayette and others, to have the medal designs engraved, and to help organize the French branch of the society.

When L'Enfant returned to New York in 1784, he continued to serve Washington. As a result of his design of Federal Hall in 1788-89, Washington appointed him planner for the country's new capital. His task would be to carve out of a wilderness on the banks of the Potomac River a city as grand as the country itself.

Washington wanted the federal city ready for the U.S. Congress by 1800. If it were not, he feared the site of the capital would shift to Philadelphia. That city, which had hosted the Continental Congress, stood by eagerly awaiting the opportunity to be the U.S. capital. As enticement Philadelphia had announced plans to create, at state expense, the public buildings needed to house government.

In response to Washington's urging, the young designer plotted the layout of the capital in less than three months. L'Enfant located streets, sited eight public buildings and proposed the underlying logic that would govern the city's expansion. As the site of the halls of Congress -- which Jefferson named "The Capitol" -- he pointed to the hill beyond Tiber Creek. "A pedestal waiting for a monument" he pronounced. He chose a lower position with a view of the river as the site for the President's House.[4]

Instead of laying out streets of uniform length, he designed a mix of short and long blocks. The short blocks were intended for residential neighborhoods, the long streets, for commercial and ceremonial use.

On top of his chessboard of streets he imposed diagonal avenues to connect separate and distant sites with principal buildings. Where angled avenues connected with the north-south, east-west streets, he designed public squares or circles.

The diagonal avenues allowed L'Enfant to use a favored technique of baroque city planners: reciprocity of sight. With this device three streets radiate from a single point which means the central position can be seen reciprocally from any one of the three streets. For nervous monarchs this meant that a single cannon placed in the central point could command thoroughfares in several directions.

Carroll's house, located between E, F, Second and New Jersey Streets S.E., ruined the reciprocity of sight between two such diagonal streets. Before tearing down the offending structure, L'Enfant warned the commissioner in a letter that his plan called for an open space not a private residence on the site. Carroll responded that later, when the city building program reached his site, he'd tear down his house but not before.

L'Enfant refused to wait because he believed constructionof all of the public buildings in his plan would proceed rapidly. Failing to realize that Congress lacked the funds to finance his grand plan, L'Enfant focused only on his vision. So, he ordered the demolition of Carroll's house. By the time the last brick fell and Carroll's harsh words faded, L'Enfant believed he had won his point. Adoption of his grand plan was assured -- or so he thought.

L'Enfant miscalculated. By tearing down the Carroll house, he accelerated a descent that wouldn't end until he touched bottom. L'Enfant's drastic action was but a "serious incident in a chain of troubles".[5] For a number of reason, Washington was losing patience.

* * * * * *

Even before the demolition, the three commissioners had run into their own obstacle -- L'Enfant. L'Enfant, feeling that Washington had given him freedom to design as he saw fit, insisted that his plan had to be completed his way. The commissioners, who under the law actually had the authority to approve the design and its implementation, stood their ground. Conflicts abounded.

Finally, less than one year after hiring L'Enfant, Washington sent him a warning on December 2, 1791. The president asked L'Enfant to continue his work on the condition "that you can conduct yourself in subordination to the authority of the commissioners." L'Enfant "absolutely decline[d]."[6]

Two months later, Thomas Jefferson wrote to L'Enfant after conferring with Washington: "Your service must be at an end."[7]

L'Enfant responded bitterly that no one else would be able to do the job. "The same reasons that have driven me from the establishment, will prevent any man of capacity ... from engaging in a work that must defeat his sanguine hopes and baffle his exertions."[8] The raw land, the lack of materials and personnel, the bad weather -- all, according to L'Enfant, had conspired against him.

At Washington's suggestion, Jefferson offered L'Enfant $2500 for his work; the designer refused the paltry sum. L'Enfant remained silent until after President Washington's death because he did not wish to get into an argument with his general. Then in 1800, he asked Congress to settle its debt with him; he claimed the government owed him $95,000 for his labor.

L'Enfant walked the halls of Congress, endlessly petitioning for payment of the $100,000 he thought his services were worth. Five years later, by an act of Congress, L'Enfant was paid the sum of $666.66 with interest from 1792 -- a total of $1,394.20. He took the money, but most went to creditors.

Impoverished and unable to work at a profitable job, L'Enfant lived with his friend Thomas Digges at his estate in Green Hill, Maryland. When he died in 1825, his personal effects were valued at only $45. Unrecognized as the visionary who created the city of Washington, he was buried in a remote Maryland cemetery with only a red cedar marking his grave.

For eighty years he lay forgotten. Occasionally, Congress introduced a bill for an appropriation to erect a monument to the city planner, but they all failed.

Then, with the coming of the centennial celebration of capital's founding, interest in Washington's beginnings focused new attention on its original designer. The American Institute of Architects studied the aesthetic condition of the city and recommended the development of a plan for further expansion of the capital. Senator James McMillan of Michigan sponsored a resolution to set up a commission of experts for this purpose. That commission of architects and the famous sculptor Augustus Saint-Gaudens, studied ways to enhance the capital.

Influenced by the 1893 World Columbian Exposition in Chicago, they appreciated the way designers of the fair had created a unified whole by focusing on the relationship between the buildings and the landscape. This new vision revived the ideas that had filled L'Enfant's mind.

The commission went back to L'Enfant's 1791 plans and everything fell into place. They saw that the 18th century designer had called for the Mall to provide an open vista between the U.S. Capitol and Washington

Monument. Since railroad tracks and the U.S. Botanic Garden at the base of the Capitol blocked that view, they had to be removed.

They also studied the axis that L'Enfant had created to locate positions of the U.S. Capitol, Washington Monument and White House. By extending that axis due west, they knew where to site the proposed Lincoln Memorial.

They then extended the north-south axis from the White House through the proposed Lincoln Memorial to the site that became the Jefferson Memorial. As L'Enfant might have done, the commission placed Union Station on a diagonal with the U.S. Capitol and proposed that Arlington Memorial Bridge stand in line with Arlington House (the Custis-Lee Mansion).

The commission's recommendations were published and adopted. As a result, more and more people heralded L'Enfant as a visionary and genius.

Finally, in 1905, almost eighty years after his death, Congress voted the money needed to properly honor the designer of the city of Washington.

At Green Hills Cemetery soldiers dug up L'Enfant's casket. Transferring his remains -- a handful of dust and a few bones -- to a new casket wrapped in Old Glory, they proceeded to the rotunda of the U.S. Capitol. There, beneath the dome, they placed L'Enfant's remains. The visionary city planner lay in state -- as only seven had before him. Thousands came to honor him.

Then, eight sergeants lifted the casket onto the caisson of an artillery gun. The long-delayed triumphal march, which should have been L'Enfant's nearly a century before, wound its way to Arlington National Cemetery. "The funeral procession was nearly a mile long ... streets were lined with spectators, flags were displayed at half-mast ... the cortege passed bells tolled."[9]

At Arlington National Cemetery, on the hillside below the Custis-Lee Mansion, the foremost men of the capital surrounded the grave. After the casket was lowered into the grave, all stood with bowed heads and lowered eyes for a moment of silence. Then three volleys were fired and a musician sounded taps. Reverend William T. Russell, pastor of Saint Patrick's Church, spoke of the genius who died long before his dream came true:

"... Tardy we have been in acknowledging our debt of gratitude to him who planned, the 'City Beautiful'. But at length we have awakened to a sense of justice to him .... The City Beautiful at his feet is the proudest and most endearing monument we can erect to his memory."[10]

Almost forty years later, on a fine summer afternoon in 1948, President William Howard Taft and other dignitaries gathered at L'Enfant's grave once again. This time they honored him at the dedication of the monument that reigns on the hillside today. Although military regulations limited the size of the memorial, 11 feet by 7-1/2 feet, its situation high on a hill gives it importance.

L'Enfant's marble monument overlooks the city he conceived. And just as the streets and avenues he laid out are etched into the city we know, so also is L'Enfant's plan etched forever onto the tomb to his memory.

***

Pierre Charles L'Enfant's Washington

Arlington Cemetery, Virginia side of Memorial Bridge.. L'Enfant's monument reigns (above) on a hillside overlooking Washington.

Freedom Plaza, (Martin Luther King Plaza), Pennsylvania Avenue between 13th & 14th Streets, N.W. L'Enfant's plan is laid out in black and white stone framed with paving stones incised with quotes about the District including L'Enfant's:

> "No nation has ever before
> had the opportunity offered them
> to deliberately decide the spot
> where their capital city should be fixed."

L'Enfant Plaza, 10th & D Streets, S.W., office buildings, designed by I.M. Pei in the 1960's, border a massive plaza and boulevard.

Dolly Madison

1768-1849

Fleeing Amidst the Flames

Dolly, perhaps the most popular woman ever to live in the White House, played a central role in the early days of democracy in America. By her intelligence, warmth and charm she brought people together and helped heal the bitterness that swept the country following the end of the War of 1812.

Dolly came at a time when America most needed a cultured first lady to build America's image in the eyes of Europeans. She helped changed the perception of Washington as a crude outpost to that of a polished world capital. For American women struggling to bring refinement to their primitive homes, Dolly set a standard for culture and refinement.[1]

Born in South Carolina where her Virginia parents were spending a year, Dolly married lawyer John Todd, Jr. in 1790. After Todd's death three years later, Senator Aaron Burr introduced her to James Madison whom she married in 1794.

With the inauguration of her husband as president in 1809, Dolly became the reigning social queen of Washington. Her courage and patriotism during the tempestuous days of the War of 1812 have rarely been matched.

With the invading army's cannon thundering so near the President's House on that summer day in 1814, Dolly knew what she must do. Anxiously searching the horizon since dawn for signs of her husband, President James Madison, she finally put down the spyglass. With the enemy almost at her door, she had to act on her own.

"You must be ready at a moment's warning to flee in your carriage," General William Henry Winder, commander in charge of the defense of the capital, had warned her.[2]   Dolly reread the penciled note from her husband, delivered by a frantic sentry: "the battle is lost .... fly at once."[3]

Madison had left Dolly the day before to help organize resistance against the British invaders. After years of harassment at sea by the British, the U.S. Congress had declared war on June 18, 1812. As a result, fifty-six British warships were anchored at the mouth of the Patuxent River, thirty-five miles from Washington. Of the 54,000 soldiers aboard, many were marching toward Washington.

Despite the imminent threat, Dolly began loading a wagon with things to be sent for safekeeping to the Bank of Maryland beyond the city. When her sister, brother-in-law and friends came to see to her safety, she urged them to help her save what they could.

First, and most important, came the cabinet papers and other documents including her husband's presidential papers. Since Madison's notes taken at the Constitutional Convention were the only reliable record of those proceedings, Dolly knew their value. Into the corners of the carriage she crammed the presidential silver and china. The red velvet draperies, that minutes before had hung in the drawing room windows, came next. Then they carried out stacks of books and portraits of Adams and Jefferson.

Except for the French clock her husband had given her on their wedding day, Dolly left all of her belongings behind. Rather than taking up room with her clothing and other possessions in the limited number of wagons available, Dolly concentrated on rescuing "public treasures that had already become part of America's heritage".[4]

Of all these valuables one outshone all others: the show - piece of the mansion, the Gilbert Stuart oil painting of George Washington -- "an excellent likeness of the adored first president".[5] Only the previous day

Madison had assured George Washington Custis that the portrait would be taken care of in an emergency. Now the first lady considered it her special responsibility."[6]

The heavy painting had to be removed from the wall and loaded into the wagon. But how? Tightly screwed bolts held the painting in place. Teetering on ladders, the doorkeeper and the gardener twisted and turned the screws as they tried to loosen the bolts. The screws wouldn't budge. Others tried their hands including the Madison friends Charles Carroll and New York banker Jacob Barker who came by, hoping to speed Dolly's departure.

All attempts to free the portrait failed. At last, in desperation Carroll, implored Dolly to forget the portrait, warning her that if she didn't leave immediately, she'd be trapped among the retreating troops.[7]

But Dolly couldn't leave without saving the painting, the symbol of America trusted to her safekeeping. "Break the frame and take out the canvas", she ordered. Wielding an ax, the servants chopped the frame apart and lifted out the canvas on its stretcher.

"Save that picture if possible; if not destroy it. Under no circumstances allow it to fall into British hands," Dolly admonished Barker as she handed over the portrait. Barker agreed to take the treasure to a farmhouse above Georgetown for safekeeping.[8]

Fearing for her husband's safety, at first Dolly was determined not to leave until he arrived. Unafraid, Dolly said that she would have liked cannon at every window. "But alas! those who should have placed them there, fled before me and my whole heart mourned for my country!"[9]

Finally, Dolly agreed to leave when a young lieutenant begged her. She climbed into her carriage with her maid Sukey and drove off toward Georgetown.

Less than 30 minutes after Dolly's departure, Madison and his men pulled up to the President's House. But, with news of the British marching down Pennsylvania Avenue, they had to leave quickly. Hurriedly, Madison departed and headed across the river to Virginia intending to meet Dolly and his staff at Salona, the estate of a friend.

Two hours later the British army, led by General Robert Ross and Rear Admiral George Cockburn, marched into Washington. Their first destination: the U.S. Capitol. Entering the deserted structure, the British soldiers chopped up the woodwork and piled furniture in the center of the rooms. Then, sprinkling rocket powder on these stacks of kindling, they fired rockets to ignite fires.

As sheets of flame leapt from the Capitol, the soldiers next marched down Pennsylvania Avenue to the President's House. At the mansion, Ross discovered food and drink set out on the dining table. Sitting down to enjoy an impromptu meal, he lifted his glass in a toast to the missing president, whohe relished as a captive so he could show him in England.[10]

Cockburn surveyed the objects he would shortly burn. Before torching the mansion, he chose two souvenirs from the personal items left behind: Madison's old hat and Dolly's chair cushion.

Meanwhile, frightened citizens, escaping to the Virginia hills, watched the sky turn red as columns of smoke rose over the Capital city throughout the night. From the countryside, the demoralized soldiers of the U.S.Army heard shells bursting at the Navy Yard as they lay down in fields to rest.

Madison and the presidential party saw the lurid glow from Salona. Dolly, not knowing where to meet her husband, went to Rokeby, the estate of another Virginia friend. She sat by a window watching the same hellish sky.[11]

For two more days Dolly traveled back roads looking for her husband. From Rokeby she traveled to Salona and, having missed Madison there, continued on to Wiley's Tavern. The two reunited briefly at the tavern before Madison had to leave to rejoin Brig. General William Winder in Maryland. En route to Maryland, Madison spent the night in the Quaker community of Brookeville. Here, on the following morning, he received word that the enemy was heading back to their ships. With that news, Madison wrote to Dolly to return to Washington: "Set out thither immediately."

Together with the messenger who brought his note, Dolly set out for the capital. When she arrived, her carriage rolled past the ruins of the President's House to her sister's house on F Street. She settled down and waited in the house where she and Madison had once resided.

Later she learned that a thunderstorm with hurricane-level winds had chased the British troops away. As cataracts of water poured down on them, the invading army, soaked to its skin, wanted to head for its ships. Their desire was fulfilled when Cockburn ordered their return based on his concern that a force of as many as 12,000 American militia might be reforming behind him to cut off his retreat.[12] For these reasons, less than twenty-eight hours after they had arrived, the British quietly retraced their invasion route back to Bladensburg and Upper Marlboro to their fleet. For the capital, the war ended.

Shortly after Dolly's arrival in Washington, Madison rode up to the F Street house. He was surprised to see his wife because, in a second note, he had told her to remain in Virginia since the British might return. Dolly had received his warning but ignored it and headed for Washington anyway. "The enemy cannot frighten a free people," she said as she confronted the danger and traveled towards home.[13]

By returning to the capital, she showed her contempt for the enemy and thereby boosted the morale of the citizens. Even though she arrived at a late hour, when residents heard of her return, they gathered outside the F Street house to cheer her. Dolly responded by "smiling, waving and occasionally shaking her fist toward the north, where the British had marched."[14]

Almost overnight Dolly became America's heroine. Newspaper stories told how, through her self-sacrifice in leaving behind her personal belongings, she had saved the country's important documents and prized possessions. Admirers also hailed Dolly for her courage in returning to the capital before her safety could be assured. "She was the bravest American soldier", an observer noted.[15]

Thanks at least in part to Dolly Madison, the British attempt to thwart the American spirit had misfired. Instead of people being despondent, they were inspired. Volunteers came from all along the eastern seaboard to help rebuild the city.

But with the President's House in ruin, she and Madison were homeless. They couldn't stay permanently in her sister's home. Another fitting residence had to be found.

To the rescue came the French minister, who offered to release to them the Octagon House which he was renting. Considered the nicest residence in Washington, the Octagon House had been completed just before the President's House in 1800. Wealthy plantation owner Benjamin Tayloe had built the elegant brick house with curving walls and windows, and a spacious drawing room, ideal for entertaining.

During their one-year residence, friends and visiting dignitaries crowded the temporary President's House for a season of receptions, dinners and balls. Of all the fetes staged at the residence during their stay, nothing matched the joyous celebration that shook the foundation of the Octagon House on February 14, 1815. With the end of the War of 1812, joyous celebrants ushered in the peace with wild abandon. Every light in the Octagon House blazed as friends crowded the drawing room. Guests laughed and cried, as they filled their cups again and again from the abundantly stocked punch bowl.

Two years later with the inauguration of James Monroe, the Madisons retired to their plantation, Montpelier, in Orange County, Virginia.

For the next twenty years Dolly's life revolved around her duties as a plantation mistress. She nursed Madison's aged mother, who lived on the property, read to her husband, and entertained. Numerous visitors flocked to Montpelier; at one dinner, ninety guests dined at tables set on the lawn under the arbor.

Madison spent most of his time working on his presidential papers which he wanted to leave as his legacy to future historians. He worked transcribing his notes until his eyesight failed, and then Dolly took over the job.

Before his death in 1836, Madison had instructed Dolly to see that the papers were published. Having saved the papers from the British burning of the President's House, she well knew their importance. She would devote herself to the task of their preservation and publication.

To do this, Dolly, at age sixty-eight, returned to Washington making her home in the Lafayette Square house her husband had purchased. By then the gray stone of the President's House had been painted white; people now called it the White House. With the White House as neighbor, hers became a popular spot for the country's leaders. This combined with her old friends who still lived in Washington, made Dolly again the capital's reigning hostess.

In addition to carrying on an active social life, Dolly devoted herself for twelve years to getting Madison's papers published. Without her perseverance, the papers might have been lost forever.

After pursing many unproductive discussions with publishers, Dolly offered to sell the papers on the Federal Convention to the Congress. It purchased the papers for $30,000 in 1837. But the sale of the other papers in Madison's collection took years. Although the Senate authorized the purchase much earlier, the House of Representatives failed to act. For years the proposal was forgotten. Finally, in 1848 Congress purchased the remaining manuscripts and paid her $25,000. They also voted her an honorary privilege of copyright in foreign countries, franking privilege on her mail for the rest of her life, and a seat on the floor of the Senate.

Dolly made her last public appearance one year before she died. Looking forward to his upcoming retirement from public office, President James Polk invited Dolly to attend the grand going-away party he was throwing for himself at the White House. On that evening, every light in the mansion blazed as the Marine Band played in the outer hall and hundreds packed the state rooms.

At the peak moment of the festivities, the president took "the venerable Dolly Madison's arm" and promenaded with her through the crowded rooms.[16] Dolly, in her white satin gown and turban, again greeted old friends as she had done on the arm of her husband when she reigned as first lady.

Undoubtedly, on that evening she saw again, amidst the handsome furnishings installed by President Monroe, the Gilbert Stuart painting of George Washington she had saved so many years before as she fled amidst the flames.

***

Dolly Madison's Washington

Lafayette Square Residence, (above) Northeast corner of Lafayette Square, her home from 1837 until her death

White House, although completely rebuilt and renamed from the days when she resided in the President House, the Gilbert Stuart painting of George Washington hangs in the East Room.

Dolly Madison

Octagon House, 1799 New York Avenue N.W., the home where the Madisons lived from 1812 until their retirement to Montpelier

Stephen Decatur

1779-1820

Gun Shots At Bloody Run

The brilliant exploits of this dashing naval officer at Tripoli against the Barbary pirates elevated him to hero status. Adored by the public, Decatur received America's highest praise and honors. Admiral Horatio Nelson described his exploits as the most bold and daring of the age.

Born on Maryland's Eastern Shore, Decatur received his commission as a midshipman at age nineteen. Sixteen years later he had so impressed his superiors that they offered him almost any choice of future duties. He selected command of the first squadron in the Algerian campaign and led his country to victory.

Following this triumph, Decatur was appointed naval commissioner. Returning to Washington in 1819, he prepared to enjoy his fame and wealth with his young wife. To do so, he built a suitable house for entertaining on fashionable Lafayette Square.

Although the heroic commodore had faced death in battle and survived against all odds numerous times, one year later he unexpectedly confronted a deadly enemy.

Decatur left without a word at dawn, quietly closing the heavy door of his Lafayette Square house. Pausing for a moment at the threshold, he grasped the cold iron rail. Had Susan, his sleeping wife, awakened? If she had heard him and came to the door, he would have to explain his departure. The heroic commodore, veteran of four wars, would have to tell his beloved wife why his honor demanded that he face death on the dueling ground.

Just a few days before, the Decaturs had given a ball in their beautiful home in honor of the marriage of President Monroe's daughter. At that event, as Susan played the harp, one guest noted that Decatur stood solemnly, his eyes riveted on her.

The tall and handsome Decatur at age forty-one, had everything to live for: a loving wife, beautiful home and celebrity. Heralded as "the lord of the sea" he had conquered the Barbary pirates in the War with Tripoli, distinguished himself in the War of 1812, and the Algerian War of 1815. The envy of any man, Decatur asked himself why he proceeded now with foreboding to meet Commodore James Barron on the banks of Bloody Run.

The answer, Decatur knew, went back to a fateful day thirteen years before. In 1807, while commanding the frigate *Chesapeake*, Barron was surprised by a British warship *Leopard* outside the Virginia capes. Barron's ship was so unprepared for defense that the British were able to board his vessel and to take American seamen as prisoners, claiming they were British navy deserters. At his trial, presided over by Decatur, Barron was court martialed and suspended from the service. With his passionate devotion to country, Decatur considered Barron's inaction a criminal offense; he had blemished the U.S. Navy. As a result, Decatur determined to do all he could to prevent Barron's restoration to duty.

Barron considered Decatur's opposition a personal affront. After an angry exchange of letters, Decatur accepted Barron's challenge. The two men agreed to meet on the Bladensburg, Maryland, dueling grounds on the morning of March 22, 1820.

Before leaving the house and descending the steps into the early morning mist for that fateful meeting, Decatur lingered. Hearing no sound from within, he turned, leaving his home and wife behind.

His footsteps crunched on the gravel-covered path that led from his home around Lafayette Square to Pennsylvania Avenue. As a sea captain accustomed to being his own counsel in times of crisis, Decatur chose to walk alone. He passed the White House then tramped east through the marsh and over the creek, climbing finally to Beale's Hotel on Capitol Hill.

Here he met his two seconds Samuel Hambleton and Commodore Bainbridge. Bainbridge gripped the leather case that held Decatur's bright, steel dueling pistol. As the three ate breakfast, Decatur said he did not intend to take Barron's life and "indeed, should be very sorry to do so."[1]

Together they rode by carriage a half-mile outside of the District of Columbia jurisdiction to the Bladensburg dueling ground. Vying with St. Louis's Bloody Islands and New Orlean's Dueling Green, this secluded ravine, less than a hundred yards off the main road, became known as the dueling capital of the nation.

Although dueling in England had died out after the 1815 Napoleonic Wars, in the American south and military services men continued to defend their honor with blazing guns until the outbreak of the Civil War. Over fifty pairs of antagonists shot it out on the Bladensburg Dueling Ground in the forty years the practice continued. Most often confrontations were sparked by political debate. One of the most famous duels arose from an article that appeared in a New York paper charging corruption in Congress. In the duel that resulted, between Rep. Barent Gardnier of New York and Rep. George Washington Campbell of Tennessee, Gardnier was shot but eventually recovered and returned to Congress.[2]

At the grounds beside the creek called Bloody Run, Decatur alighted. Barron and his second Jesse Elliot waited. As Decatur and Barron greeted one another with formal bows, Bainbridge joined Elliot; they measured the distance and marked with their boots the spots where the duelists would stand. Because Barron was near-sighted, the customary spacing for a duel -- ten paces -- was shortened to eight feet. At such short range the odds were that both would die -- if both aimed to kill.

The seconds took the weapons out of their cases. Bainbridge blew gently down the barrel of Decatur's weapon, cocked the hammer and filled it with powder.

Decatur determined to satisfy the requirements of the duel by shooting but not mortally wounding Barron. He would shoot Barron in the hip just above the top of the pelvis. "I must wound Barron but I hope he is not killed".[3]

Although some said Barron would aim at Decatur's hip in order to disable but not wound mortally. Others, who knew of Barron's hatred for Decatur, felt he would shoot to kill the man who, he felt, had been responsible for his court martial. Time had fed Barron's anger; Barron saw around him men, who were junior to him in seniority, becoming famous and being awarded military honors. while possibilities of his own advancement had vanished.[4]

Ordered to take their positions, the two duelists removed their cloaks. For an instant they stood looking into one another's eyes. Barron spoke. "If we meet in another world, let us hope that we may be better friends."

"I never was your enemy, sir." Decatur responded.

With these words the door to reconciliation opened. Could not two men who spoke of friendship be spared a deadly confrontation? If at that moment the seconds had spoken, calling a halt to the duel, both men would have lived.[5] But in place of words of intercession from Bainbridge or Elliot, only the sound of bird songs broke the silence. Each second had his reason for failing to stop the duel according to some accounts.

The possibility of reconciliation faded. Without being considered cowards, neither man could stop the duel. Instead, moments later, the seconds called their orders: "Gentlemen, do not fire before the word 'one' nor after the word 'three'. Now, take stations. Be ready."

Two pistols clicked to a full cock. Two arms went up and each took aim. The seconds counted: "One, Two, ..."[6] The guns fired simultaneously. Puffs of gun powder darkened the morning sky.

Barron, shot through the right thigh, dropped his gun and crumpled to the ground. Decatur stood for a moment before collapsing; he clutched his right side with one hand and with the other held his smoking gun.

Both men were shot. Decatur's bullet only wounded Barron who would live. Barron's bullet, however, glanced upward into Decatur's abdomen, severing large blood vessels.

Mortally wounded, Decatur was carried back to Lafayette Square. From his bed he gave orders that his wife not be permitted to see him, explaining that he could not bear to see her suffering. Twelve hours after being shot, Decatur breathed his last, sorrowful that his death had not been for his country's cause.[7]

The nation mourned their hero who had died not for his country but "sacrificed to honor's tinsel fame."[8] Hundreds of poems were published in major newspapers lamenting Decatur's meaningless death.

To explain his meaningless death, years later Mrs. Decatur wrote that Decatur "never had any personal misunderstanding with the author of his death. The whole affair was gotten up through malice and cowardice on the part of one of the seconds, Captain Elliot, and accomplished through envy and jealousies on the part of the other, Commodore Bainbridge."[9] ("Bainbridge, before consenting to act as Decatur's second, had been so jealous of him that he had not spoken to him for five years.") [10]

The Decaturs neighbor on Lafayette Square, Benjamin Tayloe, agreed with Mrs. Decatur's assessment. Tayloe believed that Elliot had fanned Barron's anger toward Decatur and, as his chosen second, did nothing when he had the option to stop the duel. "Elliot wanted to wreak his own vengeance on Decatur for being the friend of Commodore Matthew Perry and for holding in his hands a correspondence intrusted to him (by Perry) that reflected severely upon Elliot."[11]

The effects of the tragedy lingered. People more than ever questioned the dueling custom. As a result, President Zachary Taylor outlawed dueling in the military. The Decatur - Barron duel was the last fought between navy captains. Men of lesser rank and civilians, however, continued to disobey the law as they maimed and killed their antagonists for another forty years .

***

Stephen Decatur's Washington

Decatur House, (above) Northwest corner of Lafayette Square, built for Decatur in 1818 by Capitol architect Benjamin Latrobe, still stands. Decatur died in the front room to the left. Now owned by the National Trust for Historic Preservation it is open to the public.

St. John's Church, 16th and H Streets N.W., Built in 1812, the church was familiar to Decatur as a Lafayette Square landmark.

Bladensburg Dueling Ground, southwest corner of the small Maryland town of Bladensburg at the junction of US #1 and US #50. A waterway, once called Bloody Run, borders the field.

Anne Royall

1769-1854

She Faced a Ducking-Stool Death Ride

In a time when the only role for a talented woman was hostessing and supporting the ambitions of her husband, Royall threatened the status quo. As an author and editor of two newspapers, she pointed her crusading pen at corrupt congressmen and fought for reform.

Born in Maryland, Royall began as a servant in the Virginia household of a scholarly Revolutionary War veteran, Captain William Royall. The captain saw to Royall's education and married her. At his death, Royall fifty - four and penniless began her career as journalist and newspaper publisher.

When Royall returned to Washington a second time in 1827, she came in triumph as the author of four books and with funding for more. Two years later one of her outspoken tirades against an opponent got her into trouble.

The strange contraption on exhibit in front of Washington's City Hall had drawn a crowd of curious people. Many joked about the ducking stool constructed by the Navy Yard shipwrights: Some thought of the device as a merry-go-round with its bucket seat at one end and ropes that made it spin faster and faster when pulled. Others recognized it as an engine of destruction -- a death warrant for its intended victim Anne Royall.

Royall, accused as a "common scold", was facing trial for an obsolete offense that in 13th century England called for a ducking stool submersion as punishment. As the inventor of the kind of journalism later called "muckraking", Royall had simply written the truth as she saw it. Some of her subjects, who considered her "truth" slander, sought revenge by sending her on a ducking stool death ride.

If convicted, she would be strapped onto the ducking stool built to insure her death. Her enemies had seen to that by "improving" on the conventional English model; this ducking stool wasn't lowered vertically but instead swept through the water horizontally in a circular motion insuring she would remain under water longer. Even in the July heat, the long ride under the cold water of the Potomac River would likely kill her.[1]

But, Royall saw the weakness of her enemies' case. Convinced the trial would vindicate her, she walked fearlessly down to City Hall to confront the ducking stool. She would escape its fatal sentence -- even if she had to call on her friends in the Jackson administration.

Curious like everyone else, she jointed the crowd at City Hall. She examined the ducking stool carefully and asked for a demonstration. Then, feigning admiration for its builders, she asked "Who would have expected the Navy Yard, which built so few ships, would have the talent to build this new iron maiden," she scoffed. "Too bad the shipwrights couldn't do the job they were paid to do, painting rotting ships and building new ones."[2]

If Royall was nervous about the possibility of actually having to ride the ducking stool, she didn't let on -- even when her enemies claimed they had no reason to wait for official sanction. They said that since Royall was guilty, and might escape the punishment, they should take matters into their own hands: "We'll get a hold of her, tie her in the chair and give her a nice cold bath in the Potomac River," suggested Dr. Ezra Stiles Ely, head of the American Presbyterian Church.[3]

Ely claimed, as his pretext for punishing Royall, that she had harassed the congregation that worshiped a few doors from her Capitol Hill dwelling. The real reason for Ely's anger ran much deeper. He hated Royall because of her free thought theories, her defense of freemasonry and her success in blocking his religious and political schemes. Ely said that he "would cut her throat and devour her and his God would help him do it."[4]

Most importantly Ely wanted to destroy her because Royall had discovered the shocking truth: Ely, the leader of the Presbyterian Church, was in collusion with the president of Second Bank of the United States. Their financial association had spawned a conspiracy that infiltrated government on all levels, in all offices. Instead of being distinctly separate, church and state were allied. The repercussions were enormous.

Ely determined to stop Royall from her expose. But rather than filing hundreds of actions against her in the courts and legislatures of many states, he focused solely on Washington, D.C. because it was unique; with its own laws and no precedents, the captal city was governed only by the U.S. Constitution. By getting the Washington court to introduce the common scold indictment, the out-dated crime would enter the federal statute book by creating its own precedent.[5] In this way the old religious crime, excluded from the U.S. Constitution, could secretly creep into federal law.

To get the common scold indictment introduced took the cooperation of the prosecutor, Judge William Cranch. Using the threat of blackmail as their wedge, Ely and his men eased Cranch into his role. A warrant was served for Royall's arrest.

To many the unconstitutional case was ludicrous, a bizarre joke. Who was this judge who lacked good sense in holding such a trial? Wasn't he threatening Royall with punishment for writing the truth?

Because of Cranch, the Jackson administration began to question the competency of all the District Court judges. The undignified behavior of judges in bringing this obviously unconstitutional case to trial had turned on the spotlight. Until this time, quietly maintaining its dignity the court had been ignored. Now for the first time Washingtonians openly spoke of the coming court reform.[6]

The Jackson administration would soon discover that using the sanctity of the bench as their veil, the court had under six administrations protected an old-boy's network of privilege. This judicial aristocracy had perpetuated a power base founded on birth and connection.

Judge Cranch, recognizing his tenuous position, struggled to find a way out. He had to carry out his promise to Dr. Ely but also had to save himself. Finally, he hit on his strategy. He would redefine American law to include English law. In this way he could reinstitute the charge of common scold and justify his position.[7]

But he had stiff opposition. Attorney Richard Coxe, one of the District's most brilliant lawyers, volunteered to defend Royall. Immediately, Coxe moved for a new trial on the grounds that the code provided no punishment to fit the misdemeanor charged. Royall's council pointed to the U.S. Constitution and its mandate against cruel and unusual punishment. In other words, there was no law to punish her for the alleged offense. With that announcement, the prosecutors howled.

The prosecuting attorneys asked for a recess then scurried around to find a law to convict Royall. Since the justice had balked at ducking her, they needed another punishment. Ransacking the statutes of English law for cases pertaining to the common scold, they eventually found a citation that proved a fine or imprisonment could lawfully be substituted for the ducking penalty. Using this information, the prosecuting attorneys pieced together a charge under which Royall could be brought to trial.

On a hot July day in 1829 the trial began. Almost every lawyer in town came to listen to the unusual proceedings. As the gavel sounded, the courtroom fell silent. Lawyers, public officials, the curious leaned forward to better hear the judge's order to Royall to come forward before the bench.

Royall stood straight and tall, approaching the judges as if she were claiming a prize. Inwardly, she must have been chuckling because later she wrote her impressions of the three solemn faces turned toward her: Judge Cranch "has a face a good deal of pumpkin in it though my friends say the pumpkin is his head. Judge Thurston "looks as if he had sat upon the rack all his life and lived on crab apples." Judge Morsel, "His face is round and wrinkled and resembles the road to Grandott after the passage of a troop of hogs."[8]

Undoubtedly, Royall bolstered her spirits by thinking about the worst case scenario: imprisonment for a year and a fine. "But no matter," she told herself. "The sentence won't stop me from writing what I think, prison or not, fine or not."[9]

Her defense mounted its attack. If it could keep the proceedings as ludicrous as possible and focus attention on Cranch's bad judgment in trying the case in the first place, they would win.

The defense called its first witness Henry Tims, door keeper of the Senate. "She slandered me," Tims responded to the opening question. The courtroom gasped in astonishment. What was a defense witness doing speaking against Mrs. Royall? Tims went on: "she said and printed it too in her book that I am very clever. I have no objection in fact I believe on the whole it is true. But she adds 'and a very exemplary man'. Now that is slander!"[10]

The court roared. The jury stifled their smiles. Even judge Cranch gave in burying his head between his hands.

But no sooner had Royall's defense chalked up one victory, than the prosecutor claimed the next. Witness after witness claimed "abominable and violent" acts committed by her.[11]

The verdict appeared uncertain when, after the closing statements, Royall rose form her seat. She spoke to the jury saying that if they loved liberty and their country, not to sacrifice both in her person.[12]

Even with her plea the jury took only minutes to reach its verdict: guilty. Although the ducking stool was obsolete as punishment, a fine was not. Royall was ordered to pay $10 and to post a bond of $100 to guarantee that she would keep the peace for one year.

The verdict disappointed Royall's enemies. They had not stopped the common scold. In fact during the trial Royall had become a celebrity. She was the heroine of everyone including the Jackson administration. During the trial "newspapers commented on the number of inner-circle administration members gathered round the common scold. "She's a good Jackson man,' declared one writer."[13]

With an eye towards her future, Royall had continued to write during the trial. By the time news of the trial reached the public, her version of it, "The Black Book" was rolling off the press; she chose the name because it was about the "black deeds of evil doers."[14]

Her enemies gnashed their teeth. Things had not worked out the way Ely envisioned. He had thought that with the jury finding Royall guilty people would ostracize her and treat her like a convicted criminal If that had happened as he planned, then the America female would get his intended message: women should stay home and leave affairs of state and religion to men.[15]

Royall lived another 25 years. As the years passed the common scold became more and more famous. Following her courtroom episode, Royall traveled for two years while writing seven books.

She returned to Washington in time for the presidential election of 1832. About the same time she began publishing the four-page newspaper *Paul Pry*, filled with local gossipy news. As she announced in the premier issue editorial of the paper, her newspaper was non-partisan. "The welfare and happiness of our country are our politics," she wrote.[16]

Her quill pen continued to "make herself noxious to many persons, tolerated by some and feared by others ... she goes about like a virago-errant in enchanted armor."[17] As she had for her books, now she interviewed everyone of importance for her newspaper. The great and aspiring also streamed to her doorway to consult with the woman who was the public conscience of the country. During this period, Royall kept in contact with every government office offering her suggestions on how problems could be solved and by whom.

Joseph Gales, Jr., editor of the *National Intelligencer* described Royall in her late years: "She wore a green calash in summer ... in winter she was bundled up in several shabby, dark shawls, or maybe she wore a cloak with a hood closely covering her head. Her face was swarthy and raw-boned and was traversed by a thousand wrinkles."[18]

Ten years before her death, she stood in a small room in the U.S. Capitol with Samuel Morse as he sent the first telegraph message from Washington to Baltimore. After walking the halls for seven years buttonholing congressmen to argue for the new invention, Royall's effort had succeeded in getting Congress to appropriate funds to test the telegraph.

On the day of the historic trial, Morse tapped out the message to his friend scientist Henry Rogers in Baltimore. Royall, Morse and the dignitaries stood waiting for Roger's response to the question "What hath God wrought?" Finally Roger's message flashed back over the wires: "Mr. Rogers' respects to Mrs. Royall."

"Samuel Morse could thank God, but Henry Rogers knew who had done the footwork."[19]

Royall died at age 85 in her home which stood on the grounds of the present day Library of Congress. Inside the Library in that treasury called the Rare Book Room, reigns her greatest monument: every issue of the newspapers she published -- all carefully preserved.

***

Anne Royall's Washington

Old City Hall, 451 Indiana Avenue N.W., (above) the pre-Civil War structure now houses the Superior Court of the District of Columbia. Her trial took place here.

U.S. Capitol. where she interviewed and lobbied Congressmen. The plaque marking the site of Samuel Morse's first telegraph message is in the small rotunda outside the second floor Old Senate Chamber.

Library of Congress, Thomas Jefferson Building, 1st & East Capitol Streets S.E. on the site where she lived the Rare Book Division preserves her books and newspapers.

Navy Yard, 8th & M Streets S.E. The iron-grille gates and Commandant's residence built by Benjamin Latrobe in the early 19th century, were familiar to her.

Oak Hill Cemetery, 30th & R Streets N.W. She lies buried here.

Peggy O'Neal Eaton

1799-1889

She Caused A President To Dismiss His Cabinet

She stood at the center of a scandal that rocked the nation. By the time the shock waves died, Peggy would cause President Andrew Jackson to dissolve his cabinet and to break with Vice President John Calhoun, opening the way for Martin Van Buren to be his 1832 running mate.

As a woman conversant about politics and the issues of the day, Peggy showed by her participation in political discussions that a woman could function as an individual and therefore must be recognized apart from her husband. Peggy, the daughter of a tavern-keeper, also battled for social equality; before her, a woman's chance of attaining social status was nil unless she was born into the upper class.

Peggy's Washington drama began when, after her first husband's death, she married President Andrew Jackson's Secretary of War John Eaton. Since Eaton had been her friend and companion while her husband was away at sea, gossip whispered they had been intimate before marriage. With Eaton's elevation to Jackson's cabinet, Peggy ascended the social ladder. Because of the rumors and her background, cabinet wives spurned her.

*P*resident Andrew Jackson infuriated by the rumors, called a cabinet meeting in the winter of 1830 to warn ministers to either treat Peggy Eaton properly or resign.

Peggy Eaton had aroused the wrath of the Washington establishment when she married Jackson's friend John Eaton, Secretary of War. With that marriage, Peggy climbed overnight to the top of the social ladder.

* * * * *

The arbiters of Washington society asked, should a tavern-keeper's daughter join the socially prominent! They whispered that if Peggy's heritage didn't disqualify her, certainly her wanton life did. Although no one could prove their truth, the rumors spread that Peggy had sinned by having affairs with dozens of men. The story even circulated that before their marriage, her husband himself had numbered among her illicit conquests. Because of the gossip, those who deemed themselves 'respectable,' shunned Peggy.

Pointing to her "low-class" background, some said that Peggy, "deserved to be ostracized". Other simply whispered, referring to her as a hussy or "that woman".

The unbending cabinet officers' wives led the way. Following each other's leads, one after the other refused to open their door to the Eatons. At official functions, the wives snubbed Peggy, speaking a little too loudly about her behind their agitated fans.

Peggy denied their accusations, claiming that she lived a chaste and proper life. She attributed any unconventional behavior not to a lack of morals but rather to her high-spirited and independent nature. She admitted that she was a little reckless of public opinion and would indulge in such fooleries as wearing one red shoe and one black shoe at the same time. But her only serious fault was caring too little about what people thought of her. A failing or not, Peggy explained she simply wasn't concerned about her reputation and winning the approval of women. Men were far more interesting to her.

Beginning as a child in her father's inn, she relished the company of men. Legislators, who had left their own families at home, came to live in William O'Neal's respected inn. The inn, located near the White House, ranked as one of the best boarding houses in Washington. With the O'Neal family running the establishment, the congressmen got home cooking and a comfortable, clean room. O'Neal's daughter, Peggy, added to the homey environment, reminding many of their own children at home, so far away.

Peggy as a child delighted guests with her pretty face, lively chatter and musical talent. Under the watchful eye of her father, she entertained visiting congressmen with her songs, often sitting on their laps. During these years Peggy boasted of as many as twenty 'uncles' -- men who ranked among the most powerful in America.[1] When Peggy and her father observed proceedings from the visitor's galleries of the House and Senate, her famous friends on the floor often waved to her.

The popular little girl grew into a stunning young woman. "The soft gray eye, the light chestnut hair, the perfect contour of face and chiseling of feature, the complexion exquisitely clear and soft, a form of faultless proportions, where the external characteristics of that beauty over which artists raved, to which poets dedicated their loveliest verses."[2] A well-known poet, Edward Coates Pinkney, glorified her in a long poem; the last stanza begins: "I fill this cup to one made up of loveliness alone...."[3]

But Peggy had more than beauty. A natural flirt, apprenticed by her experiences as a little girl, Peggy felt far more at ease with men than with women and always sought male companionships. She could talk with passion and humor about political issues with anyone, regardless of his position. She also listened sympathetically as her congressmen friends poured out their concerns, keeping their words in confidence.

As a result, admirers flocked around her. Many proposed marriage, including two congressmen, the adjutant general of the U.S. Army and an official with the British legation. Some raised their swords to duel over her favors.

In the spring of 1817, she met John Timberlake, a purser in the U.S. Navy and storekeeper aboard a large ship. Although her father had hoped she would marry a senator or cabinet member, he saw Timberlake as a good provider for his daughter. On June 14, 1817, Peggy and Timberlake were married at St. John's Presbyterian Church in Georgetown.

Shortly after, as the newly-weds settled into their suite at the inn, a new resident moved into Franklin House. The recently elected senator from Tennessee, John Eaton, became friends with both Timberlake and Peggy. When Timberlake was appointed purser on a large sloop, the

Shark, and left for an extended cruise, Eaton began escorting Peggy to Senate receptions and other social events.

Soon gossips reported the couple walking in the woods together and driving through the streets in a carriage. "Eaton took advantage of every opportunity to see Peggy, and made no secret of his friendship with her."[4] Rumors escalated, culminating with Mrs. James Monroe writing to Peggy telling her she was no longer welcome at the White House.

Until her savior arrived, Peggy's social activity came to a halt as other hostesses followed suit. Andrew Jackson, elected to Congress, moved into the Franklin House and Peggy served him meals in his parlor. Jackson, writing to his wife, mentioned Peggy often, calling her his friend.

Upon receiving word in the spring of 1826 that her husband had died at sea of pulmonary disease, Peggy lived in seclusion for one year. In 1827, she re-emerged into Washington society on the arm of Eaton. Her escort became secretary of war a year later when Jackson won the presidential election and appointed his old friend to that cabinet post. The president also advised Eaton that if he loved Peggy to marry her at once and thereby stop the gossip. On January I, 1829, President Jackson's two good friends were married.

Jackson's grew closer to the couple after the death of his wife, Rachael. The president, who seemed almost oblivious to her beauty, saw Peggy only as a warm and dear friend. Their friendship grew warmer when, while attending a barbecue at the Hermitage, Peggy noticed the host missing. Venturing into the garden, she found Jackson stretched out across his wife's grave, mourning. Peggy touched Jackson and said "Come, general, you must not do this. Please recollect what company you have in the house. You must not come out here to grieve." With that Peggy saw Jackson cast his eyes on her "With a look I shall never forget."[5]

As Jackson said, Peggy reminded him of his deceased wife, Rachael, and believed she was being ostracized as his wife had been. Jackson was convinced Rachael had died long before her time because she, like Peggy, had been the victim of cruel gossip. For that reason, and because of his friendship with her and her husband, Jackson became Peggy's protector when people questioned her morality. In response, "he announced without reserve, she is as chaste as a virgin."[6]

When Presbyterian preacher Reverend Ezra Stiles Ely claimed in a letter to Jackson that Peggy and Eaton had traveled as man and wife in New

York before they were married, Jackson sent agents to New York hotels to scrutinize their registers.

Before he was through, the president produced ninety pages of affidavits testifying to Peggy's innocence. "Jackson, super-tensed to spot and avenge injustice, had at once put all of his lawyer's skill to work on the facts in Mrs. Eaton's case and virtually tore to shreds all the evidence against her -- all except mere rumor -- which in her case was all-sufficient to damn her."[7]

With the evidence before him, Jackson, using the power of his office as bulwark, declared Mrs. Eaton vindicated. Although no one agreed with him, Jackson believed he had proven Peggy's innocence. He left no room for discussion, never doubting he had changed people's minds.[8]

In addition to seeing himself as protector of a defenseless woman, Jackson had a second reason for championing Peggy. He believed his enemies were responsible for the attempts to ruin Peggy's reputation. Knowing that he would rather give up the presidency than be disloyal to friends, Jackson's foes saw an opportunity to weaken his chances for re-election. Escalate the Peggy scandal and thus harm the president because of his association with her.

Peggy also believed she was the victim of a political ploy. John Calhoun and his friends were trying to disturb the president's cabinet as much as possible. If they could anger Jackson by attacking her, the president would react and lose favor with his party and possibly lose the re-election nomination.[9]

Jackson marked the leader of the conspiracy: his own vice president, who, with an eye on the presidency, had lined up his allies: Attorney General John Berrien, Navy Secretary John Branch, and Treasury Secretary Samuel Ingham.

With Calhoun in the enemy camp, Jackson nurtured his relationship with Secretary of State Martin Van Buren. It also helped that Van Buren, a widower, had no wife to prevent him from lavishing attention on Peggy. Socializing with Peggy and Eaton, Van Buren and Jackson became closer and soon the widower got the president's commitment to tap him as his vice presidential running mate in 1836. With that, Van Buren stepped in line for the top office.

Thus, due to Peggy, the presidential candidate in the 1836 election shifted from the sure-bet that Calhoun had been to the rising star Van Buren.

Also, Peggy was useful to Jackson because indirectly through her he could opposed his foes. The president did this by waging a lengthy battle to force the wives of his cabinet secretaries and vice president to accept her. He played his trump card when he gave the cabinet his ultimatum in 1830: either treat Peggy properly or resign.

* * * * *

At that cabinet meeting in the spring of 1830, the ministers responded to the president's ultimatum. "Resign?" they asked. If John Eaton had married such a woman, wouldn't it be wisest for the president to abandon him, old friend or not? The president should dismiss John, send him to overseas duty or back to Tennessee, they advised.

"I can't part with Major Eaton," Jackson said, "those ... who cannot harmonize with him had better withdraw, for harmony I must and will have."[10]

The cabinet conceded, telling the president what he wanted to hear: they would do what they could to make sure their wives treated Mrs. Eaton with greater tolerance. Each realized the crisis he faced. Their jobs were at stake.

But to their vows they added a caveat: How much influence did a husband have? Certainly as a married man for so many years, the president understood that the husband who dictates to a spirited wife does so at his own peril.[11]

Tired of a subject that had taken an inordinate amount of time away from pressing duties, Jackson heard what he wanted to hear. Certainly now, he thought, the "Ladies War" has ended. In the president's mind, a truce had been negotiated. After all, he had made his position clear: any indignity to the Eatons was an indignity to himself, the president.

With his mind at ease, Jackson dismissed the issue. It was time to celebrate his and Peggy's victory. At the White House with the Eatons, he toasted the end of the war.

Peggy, however, knew better. The president's threat had changed nothing. Her enemies had not surrendered. The battle would continue. When at the next White House function the vice president's wife failed to acknowledge her presence, Peggy determined the time had come for a swift, decisive counterattack.

Perfectly combining humility with self-sacrifice, Peggy used as her ammunition the response she wrote to the president's invitation to dinner.[12]   In her lengthy letter she declined his invitation. "I cannot be happy under your kind and hospitable roof ... it will only be another feast for those whose pleasure is to make me the object of their censures and reproaches."

She continued in her missive to stoke the fire: "Although I have endeavored to return good for evil ... I wish that no member of his (sic) family may ever feel the cruel suffering I have."[13]

When Peggy's note reached Jackson, he "exploded; like a roaring lion, king of the den, he put the cubs in their places."[14] After a two-year struggle in which the president had spent most of his energy on Peggy's defense, nothing had changed. Matters had now come to a deadlock.

One year after warning his cabinet, Jackson sought a resolution to the deadlock. Calling a meeting he said again that he didn't want to part with Eaton and those who couldn't harmonize should withdraw.[15]

On April of 1831, Eaton, wanting to escape any further controversy, tendered his resignations. Van Buren also resigned. "The president, obliged to accept the resignation of two of his ministers in whom he had ... unbounded confidence and for whom he entertains the greatest personal regard, immediately required the resignation of the rest of the cabinet with the exception of Mr. Barry, postmaster general."[16]

Not only did Jackson fire his cabinet, but he abandoned the vice president. Since Vice President Calhoun was out of favor with Jackson, Van Buren instead moved into the running mate slot for the 1836 elections. Calhoun's opportunity to become president faded away.

After playing her historic role, Peggy continued her colorful life. First she joined her husband on his assignment as governor of Florida. Then, when John was named minister to Spain for the United States, she accompanied him to Madrid. In preparation for her new life, Peggy studied the Spanish language and culture. By the time she arrived in Spain, she spoke the language fluently. Partly because of this fluency she immediately became friends with the most powerful person in Spain -- Queen Apparent Maria Cristina .

The Spanish queen and the tavern-keeper's daughter had a great deal in common: they were both young, fascinated by power, had brilliant minds and cared little what the world thought of their doings. As friends, the two spent long hours together, usually alone. Sometimes they even locked the doors and indulged in a forbidden pleasure: smoking Spanish cigars!

At such times, Peggy had Maria's ear, Because she did, Peggy quickly became the most influential person in Madrid. Those who wanted favors from Maria first tried to win Peggy's cooperation in presenting their case. Following her instincts, however, Peggy refused to play a game of subterfuge; instead she told Maria everything with witty descriptions of the fawning mien of those who had approached her. The two friends laughed.

Peggy kept her friendship and also accommodated those who asked for her help. For by telling Maria the truth, she indirectly also brought issues to the queen's attention.

At the end of their assignment in Madrid, Peggy and John returned to New York and eventually to Washington. After John Eaton's death in 1856, Peggy shut herself off from the world for one year. After that mourning period, she accepted her first invitation. She would make her dramatic return to Washington society. The scene was once again the President's House but this time she reigned as dinner party hostess for her old friend President James Buchanan.

Peggy must have felt quite at home in the famous mansion. She had been there numerous times in her long life, the guest of seven presidents. Under a new administration in a new era, times had changed. The unpleasantness of the past faded. Peggy had outlived many of her enemies, and those who remained had, quite simply, lost interest in battling her.

But some things remained the same. Peggy still attracted the attention of men. Rumor now had it that President Buchanan himself wished to court her.

Even as a woman of eighty-five, Peggy lingered in the memory of one man: "She was old, though sprightly and vivacious and there was a charm in her way of speaking and in the expression of her face and in her gestures ... she was fascinating. Her hair was white, but her eyes were bright and merry, and her voice was still clear and musical. It was still the voice of a young woman."[17]

Shortly before her death, a journalist writing for the *National Republican* summed up Peggy in words that she would have loved: He wrote that she had "... pluck, hauteur, quality and blood, she cared for Number One, and if we were unfortunate enough to be a woman, we would hesitate, even now, about a collision with her."

***

Peggy Eaton's Washington

White House, (in the background) where she frequently visited as the guest of presidents Andrew Jackson and James Buchanan. The 1853 bronze statue of her champion, Andrew Jackson, was the first equestrian figure in the United States.

U.S. Capitol, where she was wheeled around by her father before she could walk and throughout her later life climbed to the visitor's galleries to witness proceedings in both the House and Senate.

St. John's Episcopal Church, Georgetown, where she and Timberlake were married.

Franklin House, 21st & I Streets N.W., site of the O'Neal family tavern.

Oak Hill Cemetery, 30th & R Streets N.W., where she lies buried beside the grave of her husband John Eaton.

Emily and Mary Edmondson
1848

Escape to Freedom

Seventeen years before the abolition of slavery in America, seventy-seven men, women and children enslaved in the nation's capital risked their lives in their quest for freedom. Boarding the schooner Pearl in Washington harbor, they began a journey that changed the world.

Through a book written by one of their descendents the story of two of these passengers survives. It tells a story of bitter despair and of transcendent joy.

For one moment, Daniel Bell forgot his race and his subservient position as a black man. Swept away by the thought that freedom belonged to all men, he cheered and applauded Senator Henry Foote's words.

Daniel, a freed black, stood with his two slave friends Samuel Edmondson and Paul Jennings on the edge of Lafayette Square. They had joined the festive crowd on a spring day in 1848 celebrating the triumph for freedom that the French had won in deposing their king and proclaiming France a republic.

"That man made me forget my color the way he talked," Daniel explained when Paul anxiously pulled him by his coat sleeve.

Although less vociferous in their feelings, the others agreed with Daniel. Each was excited by the senator's speech, which linked the French victory for liberty with America's dawning period "of the universal emancipation of man from the fetters of civil oppression ...."[1] The black men asked if the words meant that universal liberty extended beyond the white race and included the black man? Would black men and women be delivered from slavery?

Concerned about the attention Daniel's outburst had drawn, Samuel cautioned: "It won't do us to let the white people know we realize the force of what has been said for they'll say right away 'them niggers need watching'!"

Shaking their heads in agreement, the three friends walked quickly away from the square. When they arrived at a safe spot, Paul voiced what each man felt: "There's Senator Foote and all the rest of them rejoicing that liberty and freedom from oppression have come to people thousands of miles away, while right here under the very sound of their voices, is a race of people whom they themselves are holding in the very worst sort of human slavery".[2]

As blacks, the three men would not be truly free until slavery was abolished throughout the country. But until that happened, they dreamed of escape to a free state. The District was a slave territory. Even if they were freed as Daniel was, their papers could be destroyed and they could be re-enslaved. Whether freed or in bondage, the blacks had no control over their fate in Washington or in any other slave state.

As they talked, each agreed it was time to do something about his situation. But what to do? Thinking of Nat Turner's failed attempt at rebellion, they agreed that fighting was out of the question. The next obvious option running away seemed impossible until Paul spoke.

While staying at a Baltimore hotel with his master, he had met a schooner captain named Daniel Drayton. Drayton, born in New Jersey, sailed a cargo vessel named the *Pearl* up and down the Chesapeake Bay. During their long conversation, the captain told Paul that he sympathized with black men's plight and wanted to assist in their quest for freedom.

In his early years, Drayton thought negroes only fit to be slaves and had turned a deaf ear to their constant requests for passage to free northern states. Gradually, however, the schooner captain changed his views. He learned from first- hand experience that blacks were neither docile nor stupid. He discovered that negroes had the same desires, wishes and hopes as he.

Too, Drayton knew the Declaration of Independence asserted that all men are born free and equal ... and that he would not like to be a slave, even to the best of masters. He could not perceive why the golden rule of doing unto others as you would wish them to do unto you did not apply to assisting slaves from escaping bondage.[3]

With a ship at his disposal, the captain began offering slaves a way to freedom. By sailing from Washington down the Potomac River to Chesapeake Bay, the schooner would be out of range of Washington jurisdiction. From the bay the ship would head North to the free state of Pennsylvania.

A letter from the captain that Paul pulled from his inner waistcoat pocket turned talk into reality. The message written by the captain seemingly came from Paul's brother. It asked Paul to come to the *Pearl* on the evening of April 13 at the White House Wharf to pick up "something for their mother". By communicating in this way the captain had conveyed the date, time and place of departure without risking a problem if the letter were intercepted.[4]

Enthused by the prospects of the escape, the three men flew into action. In moments they had disbursed, hurrying to inform their relatives and friends of the sailing of the *Pearl* that evening.

Samuel rushed to find his teenage sisters, Emily and Mary. Born into slavery, the two girls had been hired out to work in the homes of two local families. Like their three sisters and four brothers, the mulatto girls were distinguished both by their physical and mental development. Sixteen-year-old Emily had a graceful rounded figure and a face with strong character lines and shining eyes. Mary, two years younger, resembled more "some frail, sweet flower of delicate beauty".[5] Because of their attractive appearance the young pair would bring a high market price if slave traders got their hands on them. If that happened they'd be separated from all they loved and face the possibility of being sold to a cruel master.

Although they were safe for the moment, their mother, Milly, lived in constant fear that her daughters would be sold in the slave market and taken from her. A slave her entire life, Milly was forced to marry or face being expelled from her much-loved church. She was told that her value to her master lay in breeding children to be sold in the slave market. Thus, with no control over her daughters' fate, she warned them not to marry until they had their liberty. "Don't marry to be mothers to children that 'ain't your own," she had admonished.[6]

Because of their mother's passionate words, Emily and Mary placed high priority on winning their freedom. When the opportunity came, they acted without hesitation. Both agreed to accompany their brother to the *Pearl* when he finally caught up with them on that April evening.

Samuel, who immediately had rushed to find Mary and Emily, kept missing them as he went first to their homes and then to those of their sisters. Finally at 10:00 p.m., when Samuel returned to Emily's home he saw a light in her window. He threw a small clod on her windowpane and whispered his plan. Readily agreeing to accompany him, the two walked quickly to get their sister, Mary. Mary hold their hands as brother and sisters began their long trek down 12th Street and across Pennsylvania Avenue to the dock at the foot of 7th Street. Along the way they stopped at a bake shop on F Street where they purchased six dozen buns and other edibles.

The schooner lay at the foot of the wharf shrouded by a light rain. As brother and sisters crossed the gangplank a uniformed man flashed a lantern in their faces before allowing them aboard. Then he conducted them below where they joined the others who had already boarded including their other three brothers.

Samuel's friend Daniel Bell was also on board with his wife and eight children. Although all of them had been set free by their master on his death bed, the master's heirs contested his will. The question of their freedom or re-enslavement would be decided in court. Since Daniel felt the odds were not good that the court would decide in their favor, he resolved to flee with his family.

Paul Jennings, who had arrived at the boat early, surprised his friends: He could not join the fugitives. Although he yearned to escape to a place where he could work to hasten the collapse of slavery, a serious consideration prevented him: His master, Daniel Webster, had paid for his freedom with the understanding that Paul would work out the debt. More than two years must yet elapse before the full amount could be repaid. For the sake of honor, Paul determined to remain in Washington. He returned to shore, disappointed.

The others settled down for their voyage to freedom.

But the little vessel traveled only a few miles before a dead calm forced it to anchor. At daylight the wind began to breeze up lightly, the captain clapped on as much sail as the craft would stand and the ship's speed increased.

Passing Alexandria and Fort Washington, the schooner approached the mouth of the Potomac at Point Lookout at sunset. But because the wind blew with such stiffness, it was impossible to go up the bay any further. Determined to wait for favorable winds, the captain ordered the anchor dropped at Cornfield Harbor, a sheltered bay often used by craft that encountered contrary winds.

Captain Drayton comforted the stowaways who were concerned about the delay. He said that unless something very unusual occurred, they would be safe from harm in the secluded bay. "Now you must have stout hearts an keep the women folks cheered up; and if all goes well, tomorrow night ought to find us tied up all safe and snug at Arch Street (Philadelphia) wharf."[7]

With his words the outlook brightened for all except two of the fugitives Emily and Mary. Influenced by a foreboding dream, Emily told Mary she feared all would not end as they wished. "It's always well to be prepared for the worst", she warned.[8]

Mary was right.

For at the same moment the escaping slaves envisioned their new lives of freedom, their masters back in Washington discovered their escape and flew into action. A posse of 100 men gathered and divided into four sections to search for the fugitives on various roads.

One group, led by a Mr. Cartwright, had gone only a short distance to the north when they were forced to a sudden halt. Before them in a cloud of dust came a dilapidated wagon pulled by a bucking mule named Caesar and driven by a freed black draysman named Judson.

Blacks kept Judson at a safe distance because they suspected him of talking too much to the whites. Judson didn't' seem to mind their aloofness because that way he didn't have to spend money on friends. He had, however, made one exception to his aversion to friendships -- he frequented the house of Emily's married sister which the young girl often visited.

One evening seeing Emily home, Judson proposed marriage. Emily laughed in disbelief, then, startled when he tried to take her hand, angrily drew away saying "You're a precious old rascal and nothing else." With that she ran away as Judson stood foolishly watching.[9]

Upon seeing old man Judson, Cartwright suspected he might be helpful. Not only did his work give him the opportunity to learn what was going on, but also he knew intimately some of the fugitives.

"Well I suppose you know all about these fine doings your friends have been up to," Cartwright said, playing into the black man's desire to win his favor -- and a reward.

I don't know nothing about no fine doings," Judson responded "but I know them niggers better had stayed where they were and got their three good meals per day and no responsibilities."

Then Judson winked slyly and asked where the posse was going. When told they were heading into the countryside to see if they couldn't find some trace of "our missing property," he grinned broadly and responded: "That appears mighty funny to me 'cause when I wants to trace anybody I try to go the same way they do."

Cartwright and his men urged their horses closer to form a solid ring around their informant. "Which way have they gone, then?" they asked in chorus. Before Judson could respond Cartwright warned him to tell the truth or "somebody's going to suffer."

"I ain't' going to tell you no lie, 'cause I's more anxious than you to see them ketched," he prefaced his reply: " I expect them niggers is a hundred miles down the river by this time ...."

Although the posse could scarcely understand such treachery, they believed Judson. Without a further word each turned their horses around and sped in the direction of the river.

As the hoof beats grew faint, Judson "executed a series of gymnastics and ended by jumping high in the air and laughing till he grew weak from the effort." Then, cracking his whip high over his head, he said: "I guess we've evened up things with them high an mighty niggers and perhaps them boys will wish they'd paid that two bits for carting their box down to the wharf too. Remembering how Emily had rejected his advances, he added "I guess that will hold Miss Emily, too".[10]

Judson's revenge sped swiftly toward the little ship anchored at Cornfield Harbor. Fifty men of the posse pressed into service one of the Dodge family's steamboat and bore down on the fugitives.

Eager eyes with powerful glasses swept the dark expanse with straining vision until one spotted a shadow blacker than all the rest. Even without a light or sound to signal them, the pursuers gradually approached the *Pearl*. Running alongside, a dozen men clambered over the sides at 2:00 a.m. as Captain Drayton and his crew slumbered peacefully. All at once they awakened to the sound of scuffling, screaming and swearing.

"We've got 'em! We've got 'em!" the voices shouted. As one of them lifted the hatch and cried "Niggers, by God!" the others cheered and banged the butts of their muskets against the deck.[11]

Below the huddled fugitives wept, prayed and fainted. Some men spoke of resisting but Emily and Mary plead tearfully for all of them to peacefully submit to their captors. They responded. Quietly the men, women and children resigned to their fate. They climbed from the hatch to the deck. The men were all bound and placed on board the steamer the women and children remained on the *Pearl* to be towed.

The procession steamed up the Potomac River to Fort Washington where the two vessels anchored for the night; the captors preferred to make their triumphant entry into Washington by day light.

The fugitives now prisoners were chained wrist and wrist together. Children wept and wailed, women shrieked and groaned. The men, dazed, stood with their heads dropped forward gazing ahead blindly. Emily's Aunt Eliza rocked to and fro with her head bent to her knees, continuously moaning.

When the *Pearl* arrived in Washington the throng of people gathered at the wharf made it seem as though the entire city had taken a holiday. People could not believe these slaves who had been so well treated would try to escape. What could have induced them to try to get their liberty? Many expressed the opinion that the slaves were a bad lot and should be sent to the Southern slave market to learn how bad a slave's live could be.

The Edmondson boys were the first to be brought off the ship. Following them came other men chained two and two together, then came the captain, mate and crew followed by the women. Emily and Mary walked calmly with an arm around each other's waist.

"Are you not ashamed to run away and make all this trouble for everybody?" a bystander asked Emily.

"No, sir, we are not. and if we had to go through it again, we'd do the same thing," she responded.[12]

As they marched the mile along Pennsylvania Avenue to the city jail, vengeful men cursed and threatened. Women and children screamed. For a few moments, before police made arrests, it looked as if a riot would break out.

At the jail a new horror dawned on the captives: with their positions changed from slaves to prisoners, their masters could sell them. The slave dealers Bruin & Hill who kept a large slave warehouse in Alexandria hovered nearby. Joseph Bruin had his eye upon the Edmondson family for twelve years waiting for the moment when they would be sold. He eagerly paid the owners of the six Edmondson children their asking price: $4500.

Then Bruin determined to sell his charges at a handsome profit. To arrive at the best financial deal, Bruin negotiated both with the children's friends and with other slave dealers. As a result in the seven months of their captivity, Emily and Mary traveled thousands of miles from the slave pens of Alexandria and Baltimore to the slave market in New Orleans. When a yellow fever epidemic broke out in New Orleans, they were returned to

Baltimore. Thrown into a series of filthy slave pens, they barely escaped the whip and the horror of being sold to a cruel master. Seasick and fearful, they survived numerous passages in rough seas on crowded ships.

All the while, their friends worked frantically to raise the money to secure their freedom. On one occasion a messenger bearing the ransom money arrived too late -- the ship carrying Emily and Mary had set sail for New Orleans minutes before.

On another occasion the girls' father, Paul, came to assure them that efforts were progressing to raise money for their release. Bruin warned him that if the sum was not raised and paid in fifteen days the girls would be returned to the southern slave markets, sold and forever lost.

The fifteen days came and went. With no word from their father, Mary and Emily resigned themselves to their fate. On the morning they were to board the boat bound for New Orleans they put on their bonnets and shawls. But as Emily looked out her cell window she gasped. The line of slaves were moving forward without either of them being called. Doubting her eyes, she pressed her face against the pane. Only when she saw the last of the gang passing through the gates did she realize the truth.

"Thank the good Lord, Mary, we are saved," she cried. Mary leapt from the corner where she was crouching and as the words sank in, she fainted.[13]

The money for their release had been raised after all. To get it their father had boarded a train for New York and went to the offices of the Anti-Slavery Society. After he stated his cause he was told that funds could not immediately be promised but that everything possible would be done. In the meantime, they suggested that he present his case to Rev. Henry Ward Beecher, the famous champion of universal freedom.

When Paul reached Rev. Beecher's Brooklyn home he broke down and sat weeping on his steps. Discovering the weeping man upon his return home, Rev. Beecher helped him into the house and listened to his sad story. But the reverend had good news. That very evening people were meeting at his church where Paul could present his case of his daughters and seek funds.

As one participant who attended the meeting reported, "I think of all the meetings I have attended in my life I never saw one that surpassed that."[14] From the pulpit Beecher set up a mock slave auction. But instead of selling the Edmondson girls into slavery those assembled bid for the purchase of their freedom. More than $220 was raised in less than half an hour.

Paul returned to Washington the next day with money, proceeded directly to Bruin's place where Emily and Mary seeing him from the window rushed wildly into the street. A few moments later with papers signed and money paid, the girls were free.

The girls were so impatient to return to their family that they asked their father to hire a carriage. When the clatter of hoofs and rumbling wheels broke the stillness of Washington's West End section, windows flew up and doors swung open. At their sister's home their mother and other relatives waited -- the family joyously reunited. The girls glowed with happiness. [15]

Because of their fame following the evening at Rev. Beecher's church, people donated funds for the education of the girls. But Mary, unable to overcome the effects of the exposure while in the slave prison, died during the first year of school.

Emily, grief stricken, left school.[16] She returned to Washington where she assisted Myrtilla Miner, a white teacher from New York committed to teaching young slaves at her Colored Girls School. The school, which once stood in the block bounded by 19th, 20th, N and O Streets N.W., later became Miner Teachers College, now part of the University of District of Columbia.

During the quiet remainder of her life Emily lived with her family in a little cabin on the grounds of the school.

As for the other slaves on the *Pearl*, those who survived, finally escaped to freedom in 1865 with the ratification of an amendment to the Constitution forever prohibiting slavery.

Although they failed to make their escape on the Pearl, in a larger sense their attempt was a triumph. For, perhaps no other event had a great influence on strengthening the abolitionist forces than the *Pearl* affair. At a meeting of the American Anti-Slavery Society its leader William Lloyd Garrison rejoiced at the slave's attempt, because they would draw the attention and sympathy of the nation.

Most importantly, the *Pearl* incident provided plot and inspiration to an author whose word would sound the death knell for slavery. In collecting the facts, Harriet Beecher Stowe interviewed Emily and Mary. Their story as retold by the famous author helped ultimately to change the world.

***

Capital Tales

Emily & Mary Edmondson's Washington

Fort Washington, (above) 5.8 miles south of Alexandria on the Washington Parkway, where the *Pearl* anchored overnight after the capture.

Brent Home, the residence of Emily's and Mary's sister once stood at the west corner 18th & L Streets N.W.

Home of Emily's Mistress, once stood near the corner 22nd & G Streets N.W.

7th Street Wharf *Pearl* docked, foot of 7th Street S.W., then known as The Island.

Bruin & Hill Slave Pens, once stood at 1315 Duke Street, Alexandria, Virginia, where Emily & Mary were first taken.

Miner Girls' School, once spread from N to O Streets between 19th & 20th Streets N.W.

Daniel Webster
1782-1852

He Spoke -- and Sang -- From His Heart

Webster, a constitutional lawyer, politician and diplomat, above all bids for immortality as an orator. Born on a rugged farm in Salisbury, New Hampshire, Webster, urged by his father, attended Dartmouth College. From there his skill as an orator set him on an upward path.

After beginning as a lawyer, Webster won election to the House of Representatives and came to Washington in 1813. He remained in the capital for most of his forty-year political career. He served in the House of Representatives for two terms, in the Senate for three, and was appointed secretary of state by three presidents.

Whether arguing cases before the Supreme Court or debating in Congress, his penetrating logic and eloquence won him national fame. But that fame did not give him the prize he sought: election to the presidency. Although the Whig party nominated him in 1836, he failed to realize his dream.

A lively crowd packed Washington's National Theater that night in 1850. Celebrities, including President Millard Fillmore, his entire cabinet, the Supreme Court justices, and congressmen, had come to hear the world-famous "Swedish Nightingale", Jenny Lind. Among the luminaries occupying the best seats, the presence of one would be remembered long after the performance ended: Daniel Webster.

As Lind reached the chorus of the patriotic favorite "Hail Columbia, Happy Land", Webster, seated in the first row, rose to his feet. To the astonishment of the audience, in full voice, he joined her in singing. At the end of the song, Webster bowed. Lind returned the gesture with a deep curtsey.

The house broke into wild applause. Webster and Lind again exchanged gestures. The audience cheered. Webster bowed a third time and Lind again curtsied in response. Only after the tenth round of bows and curtsies did the two end their performance.[1]

Whether singing the words or speaking them, Webster spent his lifetime delivering one heart-felt message: "Liberty and Union, now and forever, one and inseparable."[2]

A charismatic man with a massive chest, leonine head and dark eyes that some compared to furnaces, Webster took on the appearance of a venerable statesman at an early age. "In his customary dress, the black, long-tailed coat with gold buttons and buff-colored vest and pantaloons, he moved through the streets of Washington ... like a revolutionary frigate under full sail."[3]

He used his bellowing voice throughout his life to preserve the Union by defending the U.S. Constitution -- the document that united independent states into one indivisible union. That dedication, combined with his extraordinary presence, voice and brilliance as a writer, brought him fame. But in the end it cost him that which he most wanted.

The man heralded as "Defender of the Constitution" became interested in government at age seven. In 1789, following the ratification of the U.S. Constitution, Webster walked into a store in Salisbury, New Hampshire, his hometown. With his entire fortune of 25 cents tucked in his pocket, he surveyed the merchandise. Displayed amidst the familiar items, he spotted a colorful bandana "printed with mysterious words" under the heading "Constitution of the United States."

The storekeeper told young Webster that the writing spelled out "the rules under which our new government will operate." Webster bought the treasure and "that evening he lay on the hearth before the roaring fire and memorized all the words printed on his handkerchief. What he committed to memory, he was able to recall the rest of his life."[4]

Born into a poor farm family, Webster's father borrowed money to send him to Philips Academy in Exeter. From there, he continued to Dartmouth College, apprenticed as a lawyer in his hometown and opened his own law practice. In 1812 he was elected to the House as the representative from New Hampshire.

During his years in Congress, Webster established himself as one of the country's greatest constitutional lawyers. He argued over 100 cases. In 1816, he returned to private practice in Massachusetts. Although he found law fascinating, at heart he was still a politician and public orator. In 1822, the Massachusetts House drafted him as their U.S. representative and he returned to Washington. In 1828, he won election to the U.S. Senate.

Then, with brilliant eloquence, Senator Webster defended the Constitution in a famous speech attacking the Nullification Doctrine of 1830. He said that states did not have the right to decide whether to obey or disobey the federal laws specified in the Constitution.

To make his point that the U.S. Constitution superseded individual states, Webster passionately declared "The Constitution of the United States is the people's Constitution, the people's government. It is made for the people, by the people and answerable to the people."[5]

Critics hailed Webster's speech, which defeated the Doctrine of Nullification, as one of the greatest in Senate history. His words became the guiding philosophy for an entire nation. For a century afterward school children memorized highlights from the speech.[6]

Overnight Webster became the most famous man in America. Hailed as the "Defender of the Constitution", headlines called him the leading orator of his age. Great crowds turned out to greet him and cheering admirers packed auditoriums when he spoke.

With all this adoration, however, the great orator yearned for the one prize: the office of president of the United States. "The longing had entered his soul. He could not rid himself of the idea of this final culmination to his success."[7] From 1830, when he was widely mentioned as a possible candidate, to his death twenty-two years later, Webster considered himself a presidential candidate.

When Henry Clay got the Whig party's nomination in 1832, Webster hid his disappointment and set his sights on the 1836 election. He believed his reputation as defender of the Constitution made him ever more popular and an obvious choice as the Whig party's candidate.[8]

In 1836, Webster lost out again. Although a candidate for his party, Martin Van Buren won the election. Once again Webster looked to the future -- the elections of 1840 and 1844. But in those years John Tyler and Benjamin Harrison robbed him of his dream. Time was running out. Had Webster lost his chance to serve as president of the United States?

In 1848, his party's leaders met to nominate one member. The Senator from Massachusetts stood out. With more than thirty - five years in politics, Webster led as the country's top statesman.

But because of the popularity of General Zachery Taylor, Webster failed to get the nomination. He saw the election of a lesser man and swallowed his disappointment. When asked to run as the vice presidential candidate, Webster had no way of knowing that his only real opportunity to be president rested in his response.

But he could not accept second place. "Considering how long he had waited for 'first place', his attitude was understandable."[9] Millard Fillmore accepted the vice presidential slot. Taylor died in office after one year; the Vice President Fillmore stepped up to the top office.

Although at the age of sixty-six he took it for granted that people were beginning to say, "He is not the man he was", Webster still wanted the presidency.[10] He believed his turn would come in 1852.

And well it might, except for one thing. Established as the proponent of the Constitution and a strong national government, the great orator backed himself into a corner.[11] His defense of the Constitution, during a soon to be famous Seventh of March speech, stopped him.

The eloquent Seventh of March speech in support of the compromise proposal, addressed the problem arising with the addition of vast western territories after the Mexican War. With the these new states, the stage was set for one of the great dramas in the history of the Congress.[12] The compromise proposed by Senator Henry Clay sought to resolve the conflict between free and slave states who both wanted to claim the new territories. The struggle boiled down to a struggle between anti-slavery and pro-slavery senators. Once again, they raised the question: which is superior the state or the Constitution?

Webster worried that the endless debate over these issues that had plagued Congress for months might eventually erode the nation and even dissolve the Union. He wondered if such unresolved animosity might even lead to a civil war?

Since Webster believed no issue more pressing than the continued existence of the Union, he aligned himself with those against states' rights. Webster spoke for three hours defending that solution to the conflict, The Compromise of 1850.

His eloquence once again had a strong impact on the country; people saw themselves differently after the speech. "He was able to evoke the American consciousness of belonging together ... by pointing to the Constitution as the enduring symbol of nationhood."[13] He helped "... multitudes discover their identity as Americans."[14]

But although Webster got the credit for tipping the scale in favor of passage of the compromise proposal, he lost his chance at the presidential nomination for 1852. By backing the compromise proposal, he had staked his future on a policy that had little appeal for voters. When the issues were tariff and internal improvements, his message of devotion to the Union and obedience to laws were irrelevant. By 1852, things had changed. People wanted leaders who spoke to their specific needs as they built cities and railroads.[15]

Webster could not change with the times and talk about traditional issues. If he had, he would have lost his credibility. He had spent his life arguing that preservation of the Union was the paramount issue; if he shifted his focus politically he would shatter his image as a statesman.

Webster died without ever knowing who won his party's nomination for the presidential election of 1852.

About the time of his passing, a young lawyer in Illinois read his Seventh of March speech and took to heart the message about the meaning and importance of preserving the Union. Webster's principles guided and inspired Abraham Lincoln. In Lincoln's Gettysburg Address, Webster's words echo across time: "Government of the people, by the people and for the people."[16]

***

Daniel Webster's Washington

Webster Statue, (above) presented to the city in 1900, dominates the triangular park on west side of Scott Circle N.W.

National Theater, 1325 E Street N.W. Since 1835 six successive buildings have occupied the site.

Lafayette Square Residence on site of U.S. Chamber of Commerce. The house was presented to him when he became Secretary of State in 1841; he later sold it to W.W. Corcoran..

U.S. Capitol, original Senate Chamber on ground floor where he delivered his famous speeches including the Compromise of 1850 speech of March 7.

Mary Custis Lee
1807-1873

Roses & Tombstones

Wife, mother, and mistress of Arlington House, Mary Custis Lee ranks as one of the leading ladies of early Washington life. As the wife of Robert E. Lee, whom she married in 1831, she played an important -- though indirect -- role on our nation's history.

Though confined to a wheelchair from age thirty, Mary did not withdraw from life. Instead she aided her husband's success by creating a gracious home that became a social center. Trained by fine tutors and influenced by her intellectual father, she also had the knowledge and wisdom to be both a guide and friend to her husband.

Mary's story is also the chronicle of her famous residence which, as a memorial to George Washington, sheltered his possessions. Alone, watching the Civil War creep towards her doorstep, she was forced to flee and ultimately lost her home forever. A vengeful enemy and deceitful government officials play their parts in this unforgettable tale of a plantation and its courageous mistress.

No matter what, she would return, Mary Custis Lee vowed as her carriage wound down the road from her hilltop home to the banks of the Potomac River. As the branches of roses brushed her passing carriage, Mary looked back wistfully at Arlington House, the 1100-acre plantation home she had lived in since birth.

Her father, George Washington Custis, had built the showy plantation house to resemble an Atheninan temple. From almost anywhere in Washington, one could see the white edifice with its triangular roof and massive columns. The backdrop of hills and fringe of oak and chestnut trees added to its majesty.

Those who crossed the river to Arlington House were rewarded with views of the emerging capital city. The breathtaking vista made one think the city had been laid out specifically to be seen from the portico.

As she left Arlington House on a spring day in 1861, in her mind's eye Mary walked again inside the walls of the house. Mary's father had built the residence not only to house his family but also to exhibit the relics he had purchased from his grandfather's Mount Vernon estate. He intended that Arlington House should keep alive the nation's appreciation of his illustrious relative after his death. Her father had told Mary that she, as George Washington's only heir, would be responsible for the preservation of the memorial.

Growing up amidst the Washington relics her father so cherished, Mary had poured punch into the heirloom punch bowl with its tall sailing ship painted inside when Sam Houston had come to call. She had seen the bed in which Washington died and stood inside the tent that the General used at Yorktown -- a treasure her father occasionally set up for visitors. Sometimes visitors to Arlington were famous men. To these George often gave souvenirs: General Lafayette received George Washington's umbrella and President Andrew Jackson, his pocket telescope.

Since many visitors made a pilgrimage to the house to see the First President's possessions, Mary often heard the stories her father told about life at Mount Vernon and the Washingtons. She remembered, too, that when her father spotted picnickers and bathers at the spring at the base of the property, he would send refreshments via the servants. Sometimes he himself would ride down the hill with his violin and serenade the unexpected guests.

Mary, the only surviving child of four born to George Washington Park and Mary Lee Fitzhugh Custis, was raised with all the luxuries a young girl could desire. In the home schoolroom the best tutors came to instruct her. Her father, who in addition to being a successful farmer also painted and wrote plays, exposed her to the arts.

Her mother's garden, filled with roses, provided the fragrant flowers that her father picked each day and placed beside his daughter's breakfast plate.

As a young girl, Mary had as her playground the rolling hills and the great columned porch of the mansion which she shared with her father's beloved cats. Playmates, carefully selected to match her own station in life, came to join her. Among these was a distant cousin, Robert Edward Lee, the son of "Light Horse" Harry Lee.

At age four, in the company of his mother and siblings, Lee made his first social call on the Custis family. As the friendship between Mary and Lee grew, so did a tree they planted as a symbol of their friendship.

As Mary blossomed into young womanhood, Arlington House became the setting for receptions, teas and cotillions. Amongst the constant whirl of visitors, many a suitor sought to win Mary's heart, including the flamboyant General Sam Houston. But neither he nor the numerous others could compete with her old childhood friend, who had stolen her heart long before.

Mary was determined to marry Lee -- even though her father hesitated to bless the match. He was reluctant because of the duties that would fall to Mary's husband: he would not only be responsible for Custis' only daughter but also for the memorial he had created to George Washington. Also, George was wary of Lee's financial situation; although Lee came from a fine Virginia family, he had inherited nothing when his impoverished father died. To a protective father, even though Lee had graduated from West Point, his future looked dim. How could a young officer on modest army pay support his daughter accustomed to luxury?

But swayed by the favorable opinion of Mrs. Custis and Mary's desire, her father changed heart. When Lee called on him in the summer of 1830 and asked for Mary's hand, he consented. The couple announced their engagement. Lee returned to his post in Georgia; Mary made wedding plans for the following year.

With a wedding date set, the Custises prepared for the grand occasion. As the day approached, servants flew into action, decorating the house and preparing the feast to follow the ceremony. Mary chose her childhood friends and cousins as bridesmaids; Lee asked a few of his West Point classmates to take part.

Storm clouds burst, drenching the countryside on their wedding evening, June 30, 1831, but nothing dampened the joy of the celebration. Silver and crystal family heirlooms gleamed. Flowers from Mrs. Custis' garden bedecked the halls. Candles flickered. When the wedding march sounded, the wedding party descended the great stairway: Mary on the arm of her father, beautifully dressed bridesmaids, Lee and his attendants in their dashing dress uniforms. The couple stood beneath a graceful archway at a floral altar to take their vows.

Lee realized he had not only married Mary Anna Custis but Arlington House as well. Although his military career would lead him away from Arlington, his life would be rooted to the estate for the next thirty years.

Following days of wedding feasting with friends and relatives, Lee and Mary left to settle into army life at Fort Monroe, Virginia. When Mary became pregnant in the following year, she returned to Arlington alone. While awaiting the baby, she decided she and Lee should move in with her parents and make their home at Arlington.

With her second pregnancy the following year, Mary convinced her husband to make that change; shortly after Lee accepted a chief engineer assignment in Washington and the couple moved into Arlington House.

For the next thirty years, Lee resided at Arlington House between assignments at posts in St. Louis, Texas, West Point and Harper's Ferry. Mary accompanied Lee to St. Louis and West Point but otherwise remained at Arlington House. Her deteriorating health became a major concern following the birth of their second of seven children. Shortly after giving birth, Mary developed chronic arthritis and became an invalid. The rest of her life she used crutches to walk short distances or a wheelchair.

During this period, although Lee yearned to be with his family at Arlington, his military assignments forced him to move around the country.

A turning point in his life came in 1841 when Lee was called away to serve in the Mexican War as an engineer and soldier. By displaying great courage in battle, he distinguished himself and as a result was appointed superintendent of the Military Academy at West Point. Seven years later he was offered command of the detachment assigned to capture John Brown who had seized the federal arsenal at Harper's Ferry. The success of that assignment brought him even greater recognition.

When a war between the north and south looked imminent, Abraham Lincoln offered Lee command of the Union Army. Instead, Lee resigned his commission as colonel of the Union's First Regiment of Cavalry, and on a Sunday afternoon in April 1861, donned civilian clothes and rode off to Richmond to offer his services to the Confederacy. Although he had given most of his life to the American army, he could not fight against Virginia, saying "I have not been able to make up my mind to raise my hand against my relatives, my children, my home."[1]

Before departing, Lee tried to prepare Mary for the looming confrontation between north and south. But Mary refused to face the prospect of leaving the home she loved. When the time came, Lee kissed his wife good-bye, confident that she would do whatever was necessary when the inevitable war broke out.[2] Even his letters a few days later begging her to leave didn't stir her to action.

But an unexpected visitor did.

The arrival of her cousin William Orton Williams one morning forced Mary to face reality. As she sat peacefully painting, Mary took in the young man's warning: The enemy was preparing to cross Long Bridge; the next day they would take possession of Arlington House.[3]

Awakened to her situation, Mary flew into action. With her servants following her commands, she packed, and sent to Alexandria, the family silver, Washington's letters, papers and jewelry. The family portraits and other valuable paintings were taken from their frames and, together with the family piano, sent to Ravensworth, her aunt's plantation in Fairfax County, Virginia. Mary stacked books, engravings and other treasures into closets which she locked.

Believing Arlington, as the memorial to George Washington, to be hallowed ground, Mary stored those Washington possessions she could not carry. Convinced they would be safe, she sent the first president's camp bed and field equipment to the garret and the state china from Mount Vernon to the cellar.

With these preparations completed, Mary slept fitfully.[4] The next morning, May 23, 1861, the first battalions of the army of the north swept into Washington. Union camp fires burned among the trees bordering the plantation. Mary heard the drums beating across the river as she stood on the portico bidding her servants farewell.

Before boarding her carriage, she surveyed her gardens one last time. Never had they looked lovelier.[5]   In the garden laid out by her father and planted by her mother, which she had nurtured since their death, Mary took in the splendor of the blooming lilacs, lilies of the valley and the budding roses.

Mary left Arlington in charge of the servants and departed, like a grand lady setting out to make social calls, down the curving road. As she traveled to the safety of Ravensworth plantation, she took comfort in her conviction that although Arlington would be taken over by the Union Army, under the law it would remain her property. One day she would return.

But Mary's hopes were dashed a few months later when Congress passed a law taxing real estate in Union territory owned by Confederates. Since the real purpose of the law was to allow the government to confiscate Confederate property, it made the payment of those taxes difficult -- if not impossible. Only the legal titleholder would be allowed to make the payment in Union territory.

Even if she weren't confined to a wheelchair the trip to Alexandria was impossible. In addition, as the wife of Robert E. Lee, Mary would be arrested if she crossed Union lines. Rather than going herself, therefore, Mary used her family connections and found a cousin on the Union side. She authorized him to pay the $92.07 tax bill. But the government refused to accept the fee and, declaring default, bought the property at its assessed value of $26,810.

So, the Lees no longer owned Arlington House. Even if they had, they would never again want to live in the mansion. With the alterations being made, no Lee family heir would ever again call the estate home. Lee's enemy Montgomery Meigs had seen to that.

Although brought up in Georgia, befriended by Jefferson Davis and southern congressmen, Meigs despised all southerners even his own brother. A man of strong convictions, Meigs concept of morality told him that "rebels" against the Union were sinners because of their stance on slavery and criminals for their treason. For his role as leader of the Confederates. Meigs talked about hanging Jeff Davis and with the same vindictiveness "called Lee a murderer."[6]

As quartermaster general for the Union Army in charge of supplies, hospitals, and cemeteries, Meigs used his influence to make Lee's home as the site of a cemetery. Although the 1100-acre estate might have contained both a cemetery and a residence, Meigs heaping his revenge for Lee's misdeeds, sought to make the mansion uninhabitable by burying the dead close to the mansion.[7]

To do so, he got the Secretary of War Edwin Stanton on June 15, 1864, to designate the mansion and the 200 acres around it as a cemetery. Getting that approval was easy since Stanton "was aware of the flaws in the government's title to Arlington and therefore cast about for some surer means of keeping the former owners from ever regaining it."[8]

As part of his scheme, Meigs ordered that the dead be buried close to the house. When the officers headquartered in the mansion objected, he insisted. He even had those buried elsewhere on the grounds disinterred and reburied near the house.

Meigs didn't stop there. Two years later he saw to it that a 20-foot by 10-foot masonry burial vault was constructed in Mrs. Lee's rose garden. Into the vault he placed the remains of 2111 unknown soldiers. By the end of the war over 5,000 tombstones marked the graves of fallen soldiers.[9] He also staked out his own grave, positioning it no more than 200 yards from those of George and Mary Custis.

Even before Meigs turned Arlington into a cemetery, Lee knew the war would change the family plantation. To prepare Mary for the worst, he wrote to her explaining she mustn't expect too much. "They cannot take away the remembrance of the spot, and the memories of those that to us rendered it sacred."[10] But even with this warning, Mary wrote she could not die in peace unless she saw Arlington again.

One day in June, 1873, two-and-one-half years after Lee's death, Mary took a ride she hadn't planned. After visiting her aunt in Fairfax County and reminiscing about Arlington, she determined to see the plantation one last time.

In her carriage she climbed the hills to her old home. She was unprepared for what she saw. Even though the War Department had done everything possible to restore the plantation to its natural state, it had changed. Without the old oak trees standing guard, Mary would not have realized the land she saw before her was Arlington. A wing of the house had been replaced, doors had been altered and only empty rooms greeted her when she looked through her carriage window into the old house.

When Mary turned to look in the opposite direction, she saw the rose garden, overgrown and neglected. Beyond the garden rows after row of white tombstones stretched over the green hillsides.

Mary did not cry but she did say she never wished to see Arlington again. She looked across the shining river one last time, at the city in the distance.[11] Then she bid her home farewell forever. She died three months later.

On the day of his mother's death, her son George Washington Custis Lee began his long battle challenging the government's claim to Arlington. First he submitted a formal claim to the Senate in which he asked the government either to return his property or compensate him for it.

After the Senate rejected his petition, three years later Custis next filed a suit against the United States government. Opposed at every turn by the U.S. attorney general, Custis fought for his property for five years.

"There were moves and counter moves by the attorneys on both sides. Many important questions of law were involved; it became a great legislative chess game. The attorney-general was aware of the consequences impending; no one understood better than himself that if the United States government didn't strive mightily to maintain valid its tax sale of title to Arlington estate, it might be faced with the alternative of disinterring the remains of every soldier and sailor buried in that national cemetery."[12]

Finally, after two more years of struggling, the jury heard Custis's case and ruled in his favor. Then the government appealed the verdict. It took another three years for the case to reach the Supreme Court.

In 1882, eight years after he had first filed his claim, the court ruled that the United States had acted without due process in assessing a tax and demanding it be paid in person only by the property owner. As a result, Arlington was restored to Custis.

With that decision the U.S. government and the 16,000 war dead buried on the grounds of Arlington became trespassers. Since disinterment was out of the question, the government could not get off the land. Instead they would have to buy the property from Custis. Custis named the price: $150,000. Congress appropriated the funds and Custis relinquished his title to the United States government. With that action the one-time Custis-Lee plantation officially became Arlington National Cemetery.

For the next half century the former residence stood empty except for one wing which housed the cemetery offices. Then in 1925 Congress appropriated funding for the restoration of Arlington House and nine years later put it under the administration of the National Park Service. Once again the house was furnished as in the Lees' lifetime. The antiques, which had been moved from the attic to safer ground, came home as did furnishings that had been stored at Mount Vernon, and the Smithsonian Institution.

Today original pieces together with period copies grace the polished rooms. Outside the same oak trees stand guard and the portico frames the timeless view of the capital city gleaming across the river.

***

Mary Custis Lee's Washington

Custis-Lee Mansion, (above) on Arlington National Cemetery's highest hill, where she lived most of her life. The site, administered by the National Park Service, is open to the public.

War Department, 17th Street & Pennsylvania Avenue. On the site of the present Executive Office Building stood the modest brick building that was its predecessor. During the Mexican War, Mary accompanied her father to the military headquarters where she learned of America's victory and her husband's heroism.

Belle Boyd

1843-1900

The Siren Spy

Belle Boyd, who began spying for the Confederacy at seventeen years of age, turned her assets of youth, innocence and coquetry into a formidable threat to the Union forces. Her victims, northern men, seemed powerless to fight the feminine wiles her southern upbringing engendered. Painted as a vile creature by northern newspapers, the virgin teenage spy became a heroine -- the Joan of Arc of the Confederacy.

Born in Martinsburg, in what was then Virginia, Boyd attended Mount Washington Female College in Baltimore and made her Washington debut in 1860. Two years, later she was arrested in Martinsburg, taken to Washington by military escort and thrown into the Old Capitol Prison.

She had walked straight into their trap. Even as the eighteen-year-old Confederate spy Belle Boyd stood at her cottage door on that fateful day in 1862 she felt apprehensive. But when soldiers pulled a carriage from the coach house at Union headquarters and hitched up horses, she suspected it was being readied to take her away.

When her maid announced that two men, one a Union soldier, awaited her, Boyd's worst fears came to life. With a pounding heart she entered the drawing room and stood before the callers. The Union officer told her that the Secretary of War had ordered her to prison in Washington. The coarse-looking man who stood next to him, Secret Service Detective Cridge, would escort her.

What would happen to her? Convicted as a spy, might she spend the rest of her life in prison or even be sent to the gallows. Her emotions raged, but Boyd betrayed none as she watched soldiers strap her trunk to the carriage. As she stepped into the carriage she knew she would be watched closely by friend and foe. She resolved neither to make herself an object of derision nor one of pity. Though Boyd's heart throbbed, her eyes were dry, not a muscle of her face quivered.[1]

* * * * *

At the time of her arrest Boyd had been working for the Confederate Intelligence Service for a little over a year.

Her life as an agent had begun when her family's Washington home was confiscated by Union forces. She and her family moved back to Martinsburg just before the Battle of Bull Run. Following the battle, Boyd volunteered to nurse the wounded soldiers and heard stories about the exciting exploits of spies. Fighting for her beloved south in such a way appealed to her adventurous spirit. So, while visiting her soldier father at the Manassas military camp she joined the Confederate Intelligence Service. She quickly learned the mechanics of intelligence work, and the art of pilfering weapons and smuggling medical supplies.

To obtain information or goods, Boyd flirted and pretended to be ignorant of military affairs. Her blond hair and lithe figure helped as did "her womanly appeal, of which she had an enormous amount ... She played her own personality to the hilt, with a dramatic air and sweeping gestures, wearing rich reds and greens and feathers in her hat."[2]

However, unlike the professional female spies in Europe, Boyd's behavior was dictated by the Puritan ideal. The American version of the female spy called for a rank amateur who accomplished her ends without sacrificing her virtue. Boyd's effectiveness came from her innocence and seeming helplessness. Before her arrest, in 1862, Boyd had effectively portrayed the helpless ingenue to carry out her most famous exploits.

Her adventures began in 1861 when she fled with her mother and sister to Front Royal, Virginia, to escape the federal occupation of Martinsburg. When the three women arrived at the small hotel run by Boyd's aunt and uncle, they found Union soldiers already ensconced. General James Shields and his officers had commandeered the hotel as headquarters, forcing the couple to move into the small cottage on the grounds. The Boyds joined them in the cottage which, positioned near Union headquarters, provided Boyd with an ideal vantage for observing enemy activities.

And what Boyd couldn't see for herself, she could find out by flirting with the Union officers. Using her skills of manipulation, Boyd soon had the heart of General Shield's handsome aide-de-camp. As romance bloomed, the aide spoke of his duties. Boyd listened. From him she learned that on May 14 or 15 the staff would hold a meeting to discuss strategy. Boyd planned to join the meeting unseen

Such would be possible because on an earlier visit to the hotel she had discovered a small closet above the meeting room. From a hole drilled into its floor, she would be able to hear the speakers below.

On the night of the meeting, Boyd ran to the hotel and climbed to her perch. Almost overcome by the cigar smoke that drifted up to her, she knelt listening. She heard the men discussing their plan to trap General Jackson. At 1:00 a.m. when the meeting ended and she could safely leave the closet, Boyd slipped from the hotel, crossed the courtyard to the cottage, and enciphered a note warning Jackson of the plan.

Then she saddled her horse, mounted and rode 15 miles west to Confederate headquarters in Strasburg. She took with her the forged travel passes that a Confederate soldier had given her. When a Union sentry challenged her, she showed the pass and galloped on. Arriving at headquarters, she handed the message to an officer who assured her it would be relayed to General Jackson.

Her long night continued as she rode back across the fields and through the thick woods to Front Royal. After rubbing down her exhausted horse, she crept into the cottage where sunrise found her peacefully in bed.

Although Boyd couldn't know the effect of her message for sure, the fact that General Jackson changed his route and thus avoided capture indicated to her that he had acted on her warning.

Her contribution to the Confederacy continued when she heard of another Union plan. With their combined power, five Union divisions were planning to unite in Front Royal and overwhelm Jackson when he arrived.

But before the divisions could join forces, Jackson might surprise them. Scouts reported sighting the Confederate army only three-quarters of a mile from town, not the 50 miles the Union officers had supposed. Chaos reigned. From the frantic Union soldiers Boyd learned that if Jackson attacked before their reinforcements arrived, they would burn the stores and wagons and torch the bridges after crossing them.

Boyd saw Jackson's golden opportunity. She had to get word to him quickly. Although, through her binoculars she had spotted his location outside of town, reaching him would be dangerous.

Boyd walked right into that danger. Through the streets filled with Union soldiers, she edged her way until she reached the outskirts, then ran through fields to the Confederate troops.

As she ran, the guns trained on the road by which the Confederates were advancing blasted. Caught in the cross fire, shots and shells whistled and hissed over her head. When a shell exploded within yards, Boyd threw herself on the ground. When she arose, she stumbled, struggling until the Confederate advance guard saw her. When they did she waved her sunbonnet toward Front Royal as a signal that they should attack. The cavalry got the message. With shouts and thundering hooves they charged toward town.

Boyd next found General Jackson's aide and urged him to rush with the remainder of his force to Front Royal. If the general hurried, he would be able to capture the bridges before the Union men set them on fire.

Again, the bugle sounded and a full charge of Confederate soldiers galloped past her. As the dust cleared, Boyd saw Jackson approaching her on his horse. Thanking her for the warning, the general offered Boyd a horse for her return to town. Boyd refused his offer, saying she would not take a horse because they all would be needed for the attack. Instead, with a wave, she turned and began her hike back to Front Royal.[3]

The Confederates won a complete victory that day at Front Royal. Arriving just in time, they doused the fires set by the Union army and saved the town from destruction. Soon after, a courier delivered to Boyd a note written by General Jackson: "I thank you, for myself and for the army, for the immense service that you rendered your country today."[4]

Newspapers in the south and in the north reported Boyd's heroism. As her fame and notoriety spread, Union leaders determined to put her behind bars.

Two months later Boyd played unknowingly into her enemy's hands when she noticed two men dressed as Confederate soldiers standing by a tent near her cottage and invited them to dinner. Boyd's maid warned her that the men only pretended to be Confederates; in reality they were Yankees. But, Boyd disbelieving, played into their hands. She asked if they would take a letter to General Jackson.

Only after they left did she learn that her maid had been right. Both men were Federal spies sent to entrap her. This time she would not be able to bluff or flirt her way out of trouble. The letter was clear proof of her guilt.

When they caught up with her in Front Royal, they found her housed just across the street from their Union headquarters. The carriage they drove to her door that summer day would take her to Washington.

* * * * *

On the day of her arrest in 1862 Boyd's fears mounted as the carriage rolled out of Front Royal. As a precaution, fifty Union soldiers marched on either side of the carriage to guard her from any attempts of rescue.

Under guard Boyd rode to Martinsburg where she and her captors boarded a train to Washington. Arriving at the railroad station at the foot of Capitol hill, she was thrust into a carriage and driven quickly to the Old Capitol Prison.

The crumbling red brick structure had been built fifty years before to temporarily house Congress after the British burning of the original U.S. Capitol.

Boyd settled into her sparsely furnished cell with its barred windows. From the narrow opening she saw Pennsylvania Avenue and in the distance the home of Gen. John B. Floyd, Secretary of War in the pre-war Buchanan administration. She recalled happy times in the home, including the evening she made her debut into Washington society.

On the evening of her arrival, prison superintendent William Wood and the chief of detectives Lafayette Baker visited her cell. Baker asked for her confession, pointing to the proof of her guilt. Boyd said she had nothing to say. When he asked for her Oath of Allegiance to the United States, Boyd refused and said with passion that she didn't owe the United States government the slightest allegiance. "Sir, if it is a crime to love the south, its cause and its president, then I am a criminal. I am in your power, do with me as you please...."[5]

The other prisoners overhearing Boyd, cheered and shouted "Bravo! Bravo!" Baker grew furious when Wood showed his delight with his prisoner's spirited response.

After the two men left her cell, Boyd heard a plop as a nutshell fell at her feet. Painted on it were small Confederate flags and wrapped around it a message: "Courage, you're among friends".[6]

The nutshell was only the first in a long series of communications Boyd would have with her fellow prisoners -- even though any exchange between prisoners was strictly forbidden. Inspired by her patriotism and spunk fellow prisoners showered her with candy, fruit, flowers, Confederate flags, even a portrait of Jefferson Davis smuggled into the prison.

In response, Boyd dug holes in her prison walls and passed notes through. She even charmed the sentry who guarded her, getting him to pass messages in and out of the prison.

As the only woman in prison, the young and famous rebel spy became the focus of attention. When Boyd was permitted to sit in her doorway, unfettered prisoners crowded the doorway for a glimpse of her face. Some joined her as she sang "Dixie" and "Maryland, My Maryland" -- the "Marseillaise" of the south.

Less than a month after her incarceration, Boyd was set free as part of a formal exchange of prisoners. The federal officials were glad to be rid of the subject of daily news stories.

On the day of her liberation, Boyd lined up with 200 other rebels in the courtyard, and then marched through the prison gates to carriages for the trip to Richmond. As her carriage pulled away, prisoners cheered and Washingtonians who stood at the gate applauded.

After a heroine's welcome in Richmond, Boyd, traveled in the south, waiting for the chance to return to Martinsburg. When the town was again in the hands of the Confederates, she began her journey home. But by the time she reached Martinsburg the town had been retaken by Federalist forces. As a known spy she was placed on parole with sentries stationed around the house. Too troublesome to be allowed even the smallest freedom, Boyd was virtually imprisoned in her home. Her movements were so limited, that she could not even step out on her balcony. Months passed with no hope of escape. Then in the summer 1863, Secretary of War Stanton ordered her to return to Washington. This time the iron bars of the large Carroll Prison next to the Old Capitol Prison shut Boyd off from the outside world.

But as before, plaster crumbled as knife blades opened routes of communication in walls between her and her fellow inmates. When a board sealed off a keyhole between her cell and her neighbor's, Boyd borrowed the sentinel's bayonet to wrench it off.

Boyd also exchanged messages with 'friends' outside her prison walls. One day a rubber ball with a letter inside flew on the wings of an arrow between the bars onto her wall; instructions told her to put her messages in the ball, resew it, and toss it from the cell window.

Others worked on her behalf outside the prison walls. When, after official proceedings, Boyd was sentenced to hard labor, her father came to Washington to exert his influence. As a result of his effort, the sentence was modified; instead, Boyd would be banished to the south for the duration of the war.

Boyd first traveled to Richmond. Then, since she would not be allowed to go north to Martinsburg until the war ended, she decided to visit Europe. But hers would not be a pleasure trip. On a visit to Charleston, Boyd had learned about the dangers and excitement of blockade running. Because the Confederacy's survival depended on its exports, the north had implemented a naval blockade. To get its goods through, the south desperately needed spies, messengers, and smugglers.

Traveling under an assumed name as a private citizen recuperating from an illness, Boyd would carry dispatches through the blockade for the Confederate states of America.

After a ten day wait at the port of Wilmington, North Carolina, she boarded a propeller steamer, the blockade-runner *The Greyhound*. On her second day at sea, the Union steamer *Connecticut* sighted *The Greyhound*, chased and captured it.

Boarding the blockade runner, Union officers set the ship on a course to Boston and Fortress Monroe. Here the Confederate captain and crew could be brought to justice. Boyd feared the worst until she heard a knock at her cabin door. The young Union officer, Sam Hardinge, who entered her quarters told her, "You are a passenger not a prisoner."[7] A few days later, smitten by his prisoner, Hardinge proposed marriage.

Boyd, realizing his affection for her might be useful, hedged. She told him that because of the seriousness of the question, she could not give him an answer until they arrived in Boston.

Then she set about planning the escape of *The Greyhound*'s Confederate captain. With the understanding that Hardinge would not be injured, she agreed to divert his attention at the crucial moment. When the harbor boat which Hardinge had ordered to take him ashore drew up alongside *The Greyhound*, Boyd sent Hardinge off on an errand to his lower deck cabin. By the time he returned, the captain had climbed into the boat and safely gone ashore.

Although she had not intended it, Hardinge was arrested for complicity in the escape and was confined aboard the *Ohio*. Since Boyd was in love with him by this time, she resorted to extortion to save him. She wrote that she would reveal information about undercover federal activities if Washington officials didn't release Hardinge. In addition, revealing her true identity in a letter to the secretary of war, Boyd asked that she be escorted beyond federal jurisdiction into Canada.

The threat worked, Boyd felt, because members of Congress, reading her letter published in a newspaper, used their influence to gain her release.

Just as she had requested, Boyd was escorted to Montreal, where she joined other southern family refugees. But even in Canada she constantly ran into Union agents who followed her hoping to entrap her. As a result she sought the sanctuary of London.

Hardinge, released from detention and resigning from the U.S. Navy, followed. They were married at St. James Chapel in a ceremony attended by friends and high ranking American officials.

Boyd and her husband traveled to Liverpool, remaining together for only a week, when his ship sailed for America. On that trip Hardinge was arrested as a deserter and sent to the worst of the federal prisons, Forrest Hall, in Georgetown.

Boyd wrote to President Lincoln on Jan. 24, 1865, saying she thought it "would be well for you and me to come to some definite understanding." She wrote that if he did not see to her husband's release, she would include in her book accounts of "many atrocious circumstances respecting your government."[7]

Twenty days later Hardinge was released, so weak he could hardly walk. He managed to drag himself to New York and from there booked passage to London. But from that point nothing further was heard about Hardinge. Some thought his ship sank, others that he died before boarding the ship.

Boyd, alone in England and pregnant, had to find a way to support herself since she wouldn't accept charity. She decided to write her memoirs to earn money. She took her highly dramatic account of the first twenty-one years of her life, "Belle Boyd in Camp and Prison" to literary agent George Sala (who had published the works of Oliver Wendell Holmes and James Russell Lowell). She said to him prettily, "Will you take my life?"[8]

Sala edited the book and it appeared in the book stores of England in May 1865. An American edition followed. But even with both editions, the income was not enough to support her and her daughter, Grace.

So Boyd decided to be an actress. To learn the necessary skills, she convinced Shakespearean actor Walter Montgomery to coach her. In June 1866 she made her stage debut in Manchester.

Shortly after, President Johnson issued the Proclamation of Amnesty, her exile ended. She and Grace returned to the United States. Boyd continued her theatrical career in America, appearing in performances in St. Louis, New York City, Galveston, Houston and New Orleans. At age twenty-six she gave her last performance as an actress. A former British army officer John Swainston Hammond saw her on the New Orleans stage and was fascinated. Hammond contrived to meet her and the couple were married the following year.

Boyd had three more children with Hammond but after sixteen years they divorced. At age forty-one, Boyd married again, this time to Nathaniel High, an actor younger than herself. Her new husband became her business manager as Boyd presented dramatic narratives of her exploits as Confederate spy for another fourteen years on stages throughout the north and south.

On June 13, 1900, Boyd died of a heart attack three days before the performance she was scheduled to give in Kilbourn, Wisconsin, a summer resort 50 miles from Madison.

Her grave site in Kilbourn today gives no hint of the romance and adventure Boyd lived in her fifty-seven years on earth. For, in place of the headlines that once proclaimed her as "Joan of Arc of the South", "Siren of the Shenandoah" and "Cleopatra of the Secession", stands a little marker that says simply "Belle Boyd, Confederate Spy".

***

Belle Boyd's Washington

U.S. Capitol dome (above) was nearing completion as she entered the Carroll Prison on Capitol Hill in 1863.

Old Capital Prison stood on the present-day site of the Supreme Court, East Capitol & First Streets N.E.

Frederick Douglass
1817-1895

Triumph At The White House

Abolitionist, orator and journalist, Frederick Douglass trumpeted freedom's cause for fifty-seven years, from age twenty-one until his dying day. Born a slave in Easton, Maryland, he conceived the possibility of freedom at an early age. After escaping to the north, he worked for the abolition of slavery. He believed that though emancipation the black man would attain not only physical freedom but also social and economic equality.

With the coming of the Civil War, Douglass saw his opportunity to elevate the status of the black man. Through military participation in the war, his race would win its place in society. Guided by this conviction, Douglass worked diligently to recruit blacks until an obstacle stopped him. Black soldiers were not treated equally: they could not be commissioned, the received less pay, and, with no prisoner exchange program, they risked re-enslavement if captured by a Confederate.

Hoping to convince Lincoln that his people deserved equal treatment, he journeyed to Washington in 1863 and made his way to the White House.

When Frederick Douglass took on the "unwelcome duty" of presenting the complaints of his people to President Lincoln, he had misgivings. At a time when an immeasurable distance stretched between blacks and whites, fate directed him to meet with his country's most exalted person. Would he be told to go home? Would he be refused an interview altogether?

Encouraged by his friends to hope for at least a civil reception, Douglass in 1863 entered the White House with his acquaintance, Senator Samuel Pomeroy. Both were ushered into the president's office, where Lincoln sat in a low armchair surrounded by documents and busy secretaries. When Pomeroy introduced Douglass, Lincoln's face lit up. He arose and extended his hand in welcome.

As Douglass began explaining himself and his visit, Lincoln stopped him. "I know who you are," he said. "Sit down. I am glad to see you."

"I was never more quickly or more completely put at ease in the presence of a great man than in that of Abraham Lincoln," Douglass later wrote. "I at once felt myself in the presence of an honest man -- one whom I could love, honor and trust without reserve or doubt."[1]

* * * * *

The odyssey that culminated with Douglass's visit to the White House in 1863 had taken forty-six years. Born into slavery in 1817, young Frederick spent his first six years in the care of his grandmother. As property of the head manager at the plantation of Edward Lloyd in Easton, Maryland, the time came when Frederick had to be returned to his master.

Not until he and his grandmother reached the Chesapeake Bay plantation did he let go of her hand. After his grandmother set him down among other slave children, she slipped away without a word. Experienced in forced separations, the wise woman knew that to say "good-bye" would only prolong the pain.

In his next fourteen years as slave, Frederick's outrage grew as he saw the suffering around him. Not only were he and his fellow slaves denied the rights of family and education, but also many suffered savage beatings at the hand of their masters. As Frederick grew to adulthood he determined that somehow he would fight the evil of slavery.

His route to this dream opened when his master unknowingly assisted him in his goal: Lloyd sent the bright young slave to serve in his in-law's home in Baltimore.

As a house servant, Frederick stepped into an ideal position to educate himself. Surreptitiously he taught himself to read and write. He listened to the speeches his white playmates memorized from their school book on oratory, and as he did he learned the rhetorical method. The same book, in its discussion of the Catholics in Ireland, also opened his eyes to the concepts of equality and of emancipation.

Frederick used all he had learned when he escaped from his Baltimore master at age twenty. He escaped, with the help of a freed black woman who he later married, by borrowing the papers of a black seaman and heading north to the free-state of Massachusetts. At this time he took the name Frederick Douglass.

Gradually, Douglass began speaking out against slavery. When the leader of the antislavery movement, William Lloyd Garrison, heard the eloquent fugitive slave speak at his local church, he hired Douglass as a lecturer.

As the first fugitive-slave and lecturer Douglass recounted the horrors of slavery from experience. "Friends," he began, "only a few short months ago I was a slave, now I am free! ... Hear me, hear me while I tell you about slavery."[2]

Up until that time, a colored man was deemed a fool who confessed himself a runaway slave. But, instead of playing the fool, he made a virtue of overcoming slavery. In this way he cast himself into the mold of the self-made American and by doing so, he won the empathy of white audiences.

Accustomed to thinking of blacks as inferior, most whites were astounded at Douglass's ability and mien. For the first time they saw standing before them a man more like an African prince than chattel. Before they knew it, they were swept along by the richness of Douglass' voice, his wit and erudition. White men and women wept and laughed as Douglass masterfully pulled the strings.

As one listener reported, Douglass' speech wasn't "oratory or eloquence .... It was stormier, darker, deeper than that. It was the volcanic outbreak of human nature, long pent up in slavery and at last bursting its imprisonment."[3]

Douglass' appearance added to the impression of power: he stood over six feet, had olive brown skin, a leonine face, a mane of frizzy dark hair, and dark eyes that flashed under heavy brows.

As growing numbers heard the eloquent ex-slave speak, Douglass' fame spread. But with that fame came a hazard: his legal owner might now find, capture and return him to slavery.

To prevent the possibility, Douglass sailed for Europe where for almost two years he lectured. By the time he returned to America, supporters in London had raised $700 to buy his freedom. He came back not only as a free man but also as an international celebrity. With people eager for more of his words, Douglass established a newspaper which he called the *North Star*.

Using his newspaper and the speakers' platform, Douglass challenged slavery and racism as few others could. He rallied for international reform on two continents, wrote thousands of editorials and speeches, and published two autobiographies.

His voice grew even more powerful in the decade leading up to the Civil War. Unlike most abolitionists who abhorred the U.S. Constitution for treating slaves as three-fifths human, Douglass advocated emancipation within the political system. Instead of revolution he believed in agitation. Among other things, agitation meant putting political pressure on Lincoln to issue the Emancipation Proclamation which he did in 1863.

But because he saw racial prejudice at the root of the culture, he knew the Emancipation Proclamation would not be enough to win equality for former slaves. First, white Americans needed to recognize the black man's humanity. The real question to be answered was: is the black man entitled to the rights and privileges of a white man? To make the answer to that question positive, Douglass believed the black man would first have to fight for his manhood.

The outbreak of the Civil War set the stage for that fight and ultimately led Douglass to President Lincoln's office. With news of the first shots at Fort Sumter, Douglass saw his opportunity and grabbed it. He realized that through military participation, blacks could demonstrate their patriotism.

By doing so, they would claim their manhood and subsequently win full citizenship. He believed that although emancipation would free the slave; military service would establish his status as a full human being.

Convinced that through this action blacks could best achieve their goals, Douglass became a propagandist. In his speeches and editorials, he argued for black military participation and called on both freed blacks and slaves to enlist. At the same time he tried to convince northern whites that the Civil War was a battle against slave-holders. As whites fought that war against slavery, their black brothers would be fighting alongside them.

Douglass began a massive effort to recruit black soldiers. He appealed to the black man's patriotism, self-interest and lust for retribution against slave-holders. He told black men that by enlisting, they would prove their courage and earn self-respect. Most importantly, Douglass argued, "by wearing an eagle on his button and carrying a musket on his shoulder, no power on earth would deny his right to citizenship in the United States."[4]

Fired by Douglass's rallying cry, thousands of blacks prepared to join militia units. But they had to wait because whites resisted the idea of black soldiers. It took two years for that position to shift. Only when the preservation of the Union demanded it did the war enlarge to become also an assault on slavery. When that happened, the blacks finally were allowed to serve in the military.

Before that time Lincoln, sensitive to keeping the four border slave states in the Union, had determined not to interfere with slavery. But after two years of warfare, the administration changed its course. Only when military setbacks and weariness produced growing dissatisfaction in the north would Lincoln consent to a war against slavery as a means of weakening Southern morale.

With Lincoln's decision the war to save the Union turned into a war to free the slaves. As a result, the white man's thinking changed, opening the way for the Emancipation Proclamation; Lincoln signed the official decree abolishing slavery in January 1863.

Of course, until the south was defeated, the north could not force the south to comply with the abolition of slavery. As a result, if a black Union soldier were captured by a Confederate, he faced the threat of being sold back into slavery. Without a prisoner exchange program, the black soldier faced an awesome threat.

The question of equal pay also angered Douglass. White soldiers were paid $13 a month but black soldiers got only $10. This payment issue had drawn vehement protest from blacks as well as whites. By the fall of 1863, whole units threatened mutiny; even white officers refused to do their jobs until the blacks got equal pay.

These concerns, together with the fact that blacks were not allowed to be commissioned, had driven Douglass to request the 1863 meeting with the President of the United States. His people had waited long enough. Douglass would present the black soldiers' grievances to Lincoln himself.

* * * * *

On that day in 1863, Lincoln listened attentively as Douglass enumerated the complaints of his people. As Lincoln responded Douglass got a quick course in political exigency. First, Lincoln told him that the difference in pay was a necessary concession to smooth the way for the initial employment of blacks in the military; ultimately they would receive the same pay.

Second, he said that equal protection was difficult since it depended on retaliation. Instead of imposing such a terrible remedy, Lincoln said that if they waited the rebels themselves would stop their barbarous treatment of colored soldiers -- as they had already begun to do. Third, Lincoln conceded on the spot; he would sign any commission to colored soldiers commended to him by the Secretary of War.

Although Douglass did not agree entirely with Lincoln's reply, his trust in the president made him patient with his policies. By the time Douglass left the White House, he was convinced that justice would be done for his race. "Slavery would not survive the war and the country would survive both slavery and the war."[5]

With this change of mind, Douglass no longer doubted the ethics of recruiting black solders into a discriminatory military. Lincoln intended to treat blacks fairly; it was just a matter of time.

This conviction came as much from Lincoln's words as from the president's treatment of him. Lincoln's recognition made Douglass feel big. "His call on the president of the United States in the executive mansion itself was a crowning achievement for the boy who had once sneaked into Wye House (the Lloyd plantation mansion)."[6]

Douglass returned to Rochester, New York, where he resumed recruiting black soldiers. In June of 1864, Congress passed a bill authorizing equal pay, retroactive from January I of the same year. Due to this and Douglass's efforts, a total of 179,000 blacks joined Federal military forces in the last two years of the war. Their number made up ten percent of all who served the Union cause.

The man who had been the frustrated leader of an enslaved people at the beginning of the war had celebrated two victories at its end: blacks had been accepted in the military with equal rights, and the constitutional amendment abolishing slavery had been passed.

With the passage of the Thirteenth Amendment a new era of race relations dawned. Although the goal of racial democracy was still far away, the first steps toward it had been taken. Freedmen's schools arose from former slave quarters, some segregation laws in the north were repealed, and a black lawyer was permitted to practice before the Supreme Court.

Most importantly, Douglass' fondest dream of what might come from the Civil War became a reality. Black people for the first time felt as if they belonged in America. The war had given them a common sense of nationhood and of family. Speaking about Lincoln's assassination in Rochester, Douglass voiced that reality. He said that by sharing their grief for Lincoln's death with whites, blacks could feel a great sense of belonging. "... This touch of nature made us more than countrymen, it made us kin."[7]

Lincoln's impact on Douglass continued throughout his lifetime. On the eleventh anniversary of the Emancipation Proclamation, Douglass spoke in Washington's Lincoln Park at the unveiling of the Freedmen's Monument in memory of Abraham Lincoln. Douglass feared that the moral meaning of the Civil War -- black freedom and equality -- would be forgotten over time. To make sure the message rooted deeply in American experience, he tried to make Lincoln mythic and then link the blacks to him. He forged that link when he said that the monument not only honored Lincoln but also celebrated emancipation.

Douglass claimed for his people the right to be part of the national memory. "In doing honor to the memory of our friend and liberator we have been doing the highest honors to ourselves and to those who come after us. We have been attaching to ourselves a name and fame imperishable and immortal."[8]

From the end of the Civil War to his death thirty years later, Douglass continued to work. In 1870 he saw the passage of the Fifteenth Amendment that gave black men the vote. He became president of the Freedman's Bank, marshal of the District of Columbia, and served as minister to Haiti.

In 1877 Douglass, with his wife, bought a beautiful house on a Washington hilltop which he named Cedar Hill. From his front porch he overlooked the Anacostia River and the Capitol dome. Two years after his wife died, Douglass married a white clerk in his office, Helen Pitts. For the last fifteen years of his life, Douglass lived and worked at his hilltop home in the study that is virtually unchanged today.

Up until the end, Douglass pleaded for tolerance. The year before his death, the great orator delivered one of his most powerful speeches. From the pulpit of the Washington's Metropolitan AME Church his anger thundered and his pleading voice rang. Speaking of prejudice, he listed the ways the race problem could not be solved: keeping the Negro poor, degraded, ignorant and half-starved. He said the solution could be very easy:

> "Put away your race prejudice. Banish the idea that one class must rule over another. Recognize ... that the rights of the humblest citizen are as worthy of protection as are those of the highest ... your Republic will stand and flourish forever."[9]

***

Frederick Douglass's Washington

Cedar Hill, (above) 14th & W Streets, N.E. in Anacostia. From a rocking chair on his front porch he surveyed the capital. Built in 1878, the Frederick Douglass Museum home is administered by National Park Service and open to the public.

Douglass Residence, 316-318 A St. N.E. His first residence when he moved to Washington in 1870. He left it to move to his Anacostia home in 1878. From 1964 to 1987 the house served as the first U.S. museum to display and promote African art. Today, the National Museum of African Art on the Mall exhibs some of that original collection.

Emancipation Memorial, (IFreedmen's) Lincoln Park, north Carolina & 13th Streets, N.E. The only commemorative tribute to Lincoln before dedication of the Lincoln Memorial in 1922, the Lincoln Park memorial consists of a statue of a black breaking the chains of slavery as Lincoln holds the Emancipation Proclamation. President Ulysses S. Grant unveiled the monument on April 14, 1876; Douglass read the Proclamation and spoke.

Metropolitan AME Church, 1518 M Street N.W. Site of Douglass's last and greatest speech "The Lesson of the Hour" in 1894. Site of his state funeral attended by 2,500, including Supreme Court justices and members of Congress.

Daniel Sickles
1825-1914

He Got Away With Murder

Daniel Sickles, congressman, Union soldier and diplomat, played his most noteworthy role in a sensational tale of passion and violence.

Born in New York City, Sickles came to Washington to take his seat in the House of Representatives in 1857. With his beautiful young wife, he leased a house on fashionable Lafayette Square. Since he often worked late or traveled out of town, he suggested his handsome young neighbor Philip Barton keep his wife company. That suggestion led to murder and to a celebrated trial in which the defense used, for the first time, the plea of temporary insanity -- a turning point in American jurisprudence.

$\mathcal{F}$inally accepting the truth, Dan Sickles held his face in his hands, crying and sobbing violently. Pressing his fingers to his temples he bowed his head down as if his stomach were giving way. The fearful sounds of his moans and groans, which filled every corner of his house, "seemed to come from his very feet."[1]

Elected to the U.S. Congress in 1856 at age thirty-four, Sickles had come to Washington with his twenty-two-year-old wife Teresa. Taking up residence on fashionable Lafayette Square, Sickles became acquainted with his neighbors. Among these was U.S. District Attorney Philip Barton Key.

Since Sickles often worked late or traveled out of town, he suggested that his new friend Key accompany Teresa to social events when he couldn't. Key, a womanizer whose wife had died a few years before, eagerly accommodated his congressman friend. The flirtation that developed as Teresa and Key made the social rounds soon became a full-fledged romance. In a short time, the doors to the parlor of Sickle's home were locked as the pair made love.

Looking for a safer place for their trysts, Key rented a house on 15th Street. When he wanted Teresa to meet him at the love nest, Key waved his handkerchief from the street on the north side of Lafayette Square. Looking out the window of her home on the south side of the square, she could see his signal and thus knew when to make her way to 15th Street.

Long after everyone else knew, Sickles learned of the affair via an anonymous letter which told him: "He has as much the use of your wife as you have". The note was signed, "your friend, R.P.G." (R.P.G.'s identity was never uncovered).[2]

To verify the accusation, Sickles interviewed residents who lived near Key's rented house. They told him that a woman often slipped into the house through the back alley door but they could not positively identify her as Mrs. Sickles.

For as long as he could, Sickles held onto his hope that the woman paying visits to the house was another woman. But finally, after repeated descriptions of the caller's clothing, Sickles had no doubt. Teresa wore a large velvet shawl with twisted silk fringe and bugles, and a black bonnet with feathers and short lace veil -- the same clothes seen by the neighbors.

Knowing the truth, Sickles returned home with "a wild, distracted look" to confront Teresa. Seating her at the writing desk in their bedroom, he extracted her detailed written confession.

"I do not deny that we have had connections in this house, last spring, a year ago, in the parlor, on the sofa", she wrote. Sickles called into the bedroom as witnesses, two young women, his daughter's nursemaid and a family friend visiting the house. Both watched as Teresa signed the document on the desk before her.[3]

The next day Sickle's friend Samuel Butterworth responded to a note Sickles sent asking him to come right away. After telling Butterworth the whole story, Sickles asked what he should do next.

Butterworth said that if the whole city knew about the affair "there is but one course left to you as a man of honor. You need no advice."[4]

Sickles pondered Butterworth's words. Should he defend his honor by challenging Key to a duel? Or...? Sickles climbed the staircase to his bedroom and put his two derringers and a revolver in his pockets. Grabbing his coat, he dashed out onto Lafayette Square.

He walked past St. John's Church, turned the corner onto Madison Place and headed for Pennsylvania Avenue. There, walking ahead of him, he spotted Key.

"Key, you scoundrel, you have dishonored my house -- you must die!" Sickles yelled.

With that Sickles pulled out a gun and fired. The first shot only grazed Key. So, as Sickles raised his arm to fire again Key managed to jump him, seizing Sickles by his coat collar. As the two men struggled, Sickles dropped his gun and Key grabbed him from behind. Pulling himself free, Sickles swung around and pulled out a second gun. He fired within ten feet of Key. The bullet struck Key in his thigh.

"Don't shoot me!" Key pleaded as he fell to the ground. Sickles pulled the trigger again. When the gun misfired, he . recocked the weapon, put it to Key's chest and fired a fourth time. The bullet tore through Key's body. Mortally wounded, he collapsed. With Key groaning on the ground,

Sickles put the gun to Key's head and pulled the trigger yet again. Once more the gun misfired.[5]

Within minutes, Key died.

Sickles and Butterworth hailed a carriage and rode to the home of the attorney general where Sickles surrendered. After the report was filed, he returned to his residence, accompanied by two officials. Inside, Sickles found his friends waiting and two police officers ready to take him into custody.

But before accompanying the officers, Sickles wanted to go upstairs to the bedroom to get some papers. The officers stopped him, afraid he might harm Teresa. When Sickles assured the men he had no such intention, they let him go.

Climbing the stairs, Sickles found Teresa lying on the floor, overcome with despair. He stood before her like a statue, then said, "I've killed him." With that he turned, descended the stairs and walked out of the house, determined never to see his wife again.[6]

At the city jail, Sickles admitted he had murdered Key and asked that he be put on trial immediately.

Seven weeks later a crowd of people wrestled police to get into the dingy courtroom for the opening day of the murder trial. With only fifty seats allotted to the public, those turned away gathered outside the courtroom angrily cursing and shouting. Some were so anxious to see the congressman tried that they climbed into the courtroom through the windows. Not finding seats, they crammed into the back of the room, standing on tiptoes.

Newspaper reporters with credentials competed for space on long benches, which had to be substituted for the customary writing desks to save space. Members of the Washington bar, the diplomatic corps, Sickle's family and friends and dozens of witnesses crowded into the room.

The prosecuting District Attorney Robert Ould and the lawyer James M. Carlisle, hired by Key's relatives took their places. Eight lawyers represented Sickles: James T. Brady, master strategist of the New York bar; Edwin M. Stanton, leader of the Maryland bar; John Graham, famed for his dramatic appeals; Congressman Philip Phillips, the foremost figure of the Alabama bar; plus four prominent Washington lawyers.

In their defense of Sickles, the team of lawyers agreed to prove that Sickles was justified in killing Key because his mind had been affected by the discovery of his wife's adultery. "He was rendered temporarily insane by rage and grief at the time of the slaying." Pointing to this emotional state, his defense used for the first time the plea of temporary insanity.[7]

In the interval between murder and trial, newspapers had overwhelmingly supported Sickles. Since people believed that society's stability depended on the protection of the family and marriage, a threat to marriage was a threat to society. As part of his responsibility, a husband had a duty to defend the holy sacrament of marriage.

Sickles' lawyers capitalized on this belief. They asked in their client's defense: "What would any husband have done in the same circumstances?" Referring to Sickles and daughter, Laura, Graham elaborated: "Who would not hasten to save the mother of your child, although she be lost as wife, to rescue her from the adulterer?"[8]

"May the Lord who watches over the home and family guide the bullet and direct the stroke!", Stanton said in his indictment of adultery.

Graham summed up: "The death of Key was cheap sacrifice to save one mother from horrible fate." Graham added that it might be tragic to shed human blood "but I will always maintain that there is no tragedy about slaying the adulterer; his crime takes away the character of the occurrence .... If anyone was responsible it was Key. He and Sickles had been friends. Key deflowered the wife of his friend."[9]

The courtroom erupted into wild applause.

Judge Thomas Crawford instructed the jury that if it had "any doubt as to the case either in reference to the homicide or the question of insanity, Mr. Sickles should be acquitted." With his words the judge showed that he had accepted the defense plea of temporary insanity -- a turning point in American jurisprudence.[10]

After seventy minutes of deliberation, the jury pronounced its verdict: not guilty.

The courtroom exploded again. People shouted, cheered, kissed, danced, slapped one another on the back and wept. From the open window came the sound of the cheering throngs outside.

Freed of all charges, Sickles overcome with emotion stepped down the stairs of City Hall amidst his friends.[11] He celebrated at a reception given by his lawyer for the jury. They were "interrupted when a crowd appeared outside to serenade the defense counsel ... Sickles ... was congratulated on his victory that evening by some 1500 well-wishers".[12]

With the sympathy of the American public and his friends, he returned to his hometown in New York for a rest. Since Congress had adjourned, for the moment his work in Washington was finished. Re-elected to the House, he would return to the capital in the winter.

Three months after the trial, Sickles decided to reconcile with Teresa. Newspaper headlines screamed. The public reacted, bitterly denouncing Sickles. In response to the *New York Herald Tribune*'s suggestion that he had reconciled on advice of his attorneys, Sickles wrote a letter to the editor. He denied that he had acted on the advice of his lawyers. "I am prepared to defend what I have done before the only tribunal I recognize as having the slightest claim to jurisdiction over the subject -- my own conscience and the bar of Heaven," he wrote.[13].

The public responded with shock and anger. "Custom demanded that the woman taken in adultery be exiled from society, and for Sickles to forgive her after saving his own neck by proclaiming her shame was considered the last step in degradation."[14] Friends abandoned him in disgust.

Now, instead of supporting Sickles, people asked the obvious question: if Sickles could forgive Teresa, shouldn't Key have been forgiven and a human life spared? The newspapers made their daily assaults, asking again and again why Key had been killed and his slayer acquitted.

When Sickles returned to Washington for the first session of the 36th Congress, the members ostracized him. With President Buchanan severing his connections with him, Sickles gave up any idea of seeking reelection to a third term. His political career was finished.

But Sickles didn't retire from public life. With the outbreak of the Civil War in 1861, he raised a unit in New York and became its commander. Promoted to major-general, he played an important part in the Chancellorsville campaign, stopping Jackson's advance. In his last battle, at Gettysburg, he stopped the enemy after a slight loss of ground but was struck by a shell. His right leg was amputated in the field. With "a characteristic touch of gothic humor", Sickles had his leg placed in a miniature coffin and sent to the Army Medical Museum. He went to visit it and occasionally took friends along.[15]

His military career at an end, he was sent on a confidential mission to South America. The same year, with the war over and the South occupied, he was appointed military governor of the Carolinas. But Lincoln's successor, Andrew Johnson, thought him undiplomatic in the execution of his duties and relieved him of this office.

One year later he got a second chance when President Grant appointed him minister to Spain. But again, Sickles, weak on diplomatic skills, resigned under pressure. Before giving up his duties, however, he (a widow since Teresa's death) married a young society woman from Madrid whom he had met at the American legation.

After living abroad for seven years, Sickles returned to the Unites States -- alone; his wife refused to come with him. Not until thirty years later did they reconcile at his deathbed.

In the interval, Sickles' adventure continued. Re-elected to Congress in 1893, he served another term. When at age sixty-two he inherited his father's substantial fortune of $5 million, he devoted himself full-time to hedonistic living. By the time he died at age ninety, he had spent all the money on his favorite pursuits -- women and liquor.

***

Daniel Sickles' Washington

St. John's Church (above), 16th & H Streets N.W., he passed the church on Lafayette Square as he set out to kill Key.

Lafayette Square Residence, 722 Jackson Place N.W. where he lived with Teresa in 1857 at the time of Key's death.

Washington Club, midway on Madison Place N.W. where the Court of Claims stands today was site of Dan's and Barton's club. Key signaled with his handkerchief near the site and died within a few feet of it.

Daniel Sickles

National Museum of Health and Medicine, formerly the Army Medical Museum, Walter Reed Medical Center, 16th & Georgia Avenue N.W. Exhibits Sickles' amputated leg with his calling card "With the compliments of Major-General D.E.S. U.S. Volunteers."

Arlington National Cemetery where he's buried among his Third Corps comrades.

John Wilkes Booth
1838-1865

The Actor's Final Role

Booth, born in Virginia in 1838, was the son of a famous Shakespearean actor, Julius Brutus Booth. The handsome John Wilkes Booth achieved a lucrative acting career, touring the United States. Lincoln had seen Booth perform at Ford's Theater.

Three years after the outbreak of the Civil War, Booth gave up his acting career to serve the Confederate cause by smuggling quinine. In the weeks before the fateful night of April 14, 1865, Booth frequented the taverns of Washington, held meetings with his conspirators, and stopped by to visit a fellow actor who lived across the street from Ford's Theater.

*J*ohn Wilkes Booth, exhausted from riding his horse all day, threw himself onto the bed of his friend, actor Charles Warwick. Booth had come to visit Warwick in his small room tucked away in the back of the house across the street from Ford's Theater. On this night, at his host's suggestion, he took off his mud-splashed riding boots, hung them beside the stove and lay down to rest from his journey.

Booth slept peacefully on the four-poster bed. His calm sleeping countenance gave no hint that his feelings would cause the same bed, in a few days, to accommodate the dying Abraham Lincoln.[1]

At first the handsome actor with "deep-set eyes, black as ink and filled with a strange wild fire,"[2] had not planned to kill President Lincoln; Booth simply wanted to carry him to Richmond as hostage. By kidnapping the president, Booth hoped to force the north to release its 50,000 Confederate prisoners of war in exchange for Lincoln's freedom. Only in this way could the Confederate Army get the men they desperately needed to carry on the fight.

To carry out the scheme, Booth had recruited a gang of accomplices: David Herold, a young drugstore clerk; Louis Paine, a deserter from the Confederate army; George Atzerodt, a German immigrant who would do anything for a price, and John Surratt, a Confederate spy and blockade runner who relished danger. The group met frequently at Mary Surratt's boarding house in Washington to discuss their plans.

As an actor who relished spectacular effects, Booth decided to use the theater setting as his real-life stage. Since Lincoln attended performances at various Washington theaters, Booth's only decision was where and when to make his move.

He knew the manager of Ford's Theater and was familiar to the staff because he picked up his mail there, he favored Ford's as the site. So, when Booth learned that the president planned to attend Ford's Theater for a performance, he plotted with his two cohorts. One would darken the theater by turning off the gas that fed the lamps. The other, led by Booth, would burst into the president's box, seize Lincoln and spirit him away.

But the plan failed when fate stole the show. A violent storm hit Washington on the night of the performance; Lincoln decided to stay home.[3]

Two months later Booth tried again. This time he planned to ambush the president as he rode by carriage to a benefit stage performance at a soldier's home on the edge of the town. However, when Booth and his accomplices, pretending to be chance travelers on the road, rode by the president's carriage, they discovered he was not inside. Lincoln had cancelled his visit to the soldier's home and instead attended a ceremony outside a downtown hotel -- the same hotel where Booth resided.

By the time Booth came up with his third plan, the south had been defeated. General Grant, convinced the war was over, allowed Confederate prisoners to be exchanged for Union men. With the release of thousands of southern prisoners, Booth's reason for kidnapping Lincoln vanished. If he were to play his role as hero-savior of the south, he would have to find another reason.

That reason evolved as the people of Washington celebrated the Union victory the week of April 10, 1865, and Booth drowned himself in brandy in city saloons. As he drank, the frustrated southern patriot decided to kill Lincoln. His motive for wanting to assassinate the president may have been unclear even to himself. Perhaps he was driven by his lust for fame, by the desire of a madman to commit a spectacular murder, or simply by his sense of duty: as a Confederate spy he may have been paid for carrying out orders.[4]

Whatever the reason, Booth plotted to kill Lincoln. He made his intentions known as he stood in the audience in front of the White House three days before his fateful act listening to Lincoln speak. As part of the reconciliation between the north and south, Lincoln said he hoped the blacks would be given the right to vote. When he heard these words Booth said to his companion: "That will be the last speech *he* will ever make."[5]

Booth put actions behind that threat when he reserved a box at Grover's Theater beside the one he thought Lincoln would use on the evening of April 14. Booth would enter the box and kill Lincoln, while his conspirators, elsewhere in the city, would kill the secretary of state and vice president.

But Booth's plans for the evening suddenly changed. While picking up his mail, he overheard the manager telling a stagehand that Lincoln would be attending the performance of "Our American Cousin" at Ford's Theater that evening. Lincoln would not be going to the Grover Theater as Booth had anticipated.

Booth had to quickly revise his plans. Since, at Ford's Theater, he could not assault the president from an adjacent box, he would need to enter Lincoln's box.

With only a few hours to prepare, Booth worked frantically. He arranged for horses and rallied his accomplices: Paine, who under the first plan was to have joined Booth in the Ford's Theater box with the assignment of killing General Grant, now was told to assassinate Secretary of State William Seward instead. Atzerodt was instructed to kill his fellow boarder at Kirkwood House, Vice President Andrew Johnson.

In preparation for his escape, Booth took a package of things he would need later on -- including binoculars -- to Mary Surratt, asking that she deliver the package to the tavern on his escape route in Surrattsville, Maryland.

Then he went to Ford's Theater to prepare. In the upstairs corridor leading to the president's box, he hid a piece of wood to jam the door shut that evening.

With that accomplished, he went to his room and changed into an elegant riding outfit embellished with a new pair of spurs and concealed his derringer pistol and dagger. He next met with his conspirators to go over his latest plan a final time.

They decided that following the three assassinations -- all to take place at 10:15 p.m. -- they and Herold would meet at the Navy Yard Bridge and escape to the safety of the south.

But their plans went awry.

At a few minutes after 9:00 p.m., a half hour after Lincoln had entered the box with his wife, Major Rathbone and Rathbone's fiancee, Clara Harris, Booth rode his horse to the rear door of the theater. He dismounted, asked a stagehand to hold the horse, and entered the backstage area.

Through a trapdoor down he descended a flight of stairs and passed under the stage to stairs on the opposite side. Climbing the stairs that led to the Tenth Street alley, he . entered the saloon next door to the theater and downed a brandy. A drunken patron, recognizing him, taunted Booth: "You'll never be the actor your father was," he said. "When I leave the stage, I will be the most famous man in America," Booth responded.[6]

With that Booth re-entered the theater, climbed the stairs to the dress circle and entered the anteroom to the president's box. To prevent anyone from entering, he secured the anteroom door with the piece of wood he had hidden earlier. Then, drawing his pistol, he stood at the inner door to the box, waiting.

Since he had performed in "Our American Cousin" and had seen it a few times, he knew that when he heard a particular character deliver a certain line the stage would be empty except for the one actor. With an empty stage his chances of escape increased.

Booth heard his cue. He carefully opened the door, raised his pistol and fired at close range through the back of Lincoln's head. Major Rathbone leapt at Booth who slashed him with his dagger, wounding him in the arm.

Then the attacker vaulted over the railing and fell to the stage twelve feet below. As he jumped, Booth's spur caught in the flag-draped railing causing him to land off-balance fracturing his left leg. Despite his pain, while shouting at the audience "Sic Semper Tyrannis" (Thus Always to Tyrants), he pushed aside the actor on stage, rushed through the rear stage door, and grabbed the reins of his horse. The fleeing Booth swung onto the horse, wheeled it about and galloped down the alley into the night -- and into infamy.

Men carried the unconscious president across the street to the home of William Petersen, a tailor who supplemented his income by taking in boarders. In a rear room where Booth's friend boarded, Lincoln was laid on the same bed on which his assassin had slept in so peacefully only days before.

Lincoln lived only until early the following morning.

Seward survived because when Paine tried to assassinate him, he ran into trouble. Although Paine managed to enter Seward's bedroom and stabbed him twice, the steel brace the secretary wore around his head and neck because of an earlier accident saved his life. Johnson's designated assassin did no better. When the moment came to make his move, Atzerodt lost his nerve.

Booth rode hard to the Navy Yard Bridge where he met only Herold. Even though it was after dark -- the time the bridge was closed -- the guard waved the famous actor and his friend across. The two headed for Maryland and the safety of the south.

A few minutes after midnight, the pair arrived at the Surrattsville Tavern. They ordered the innkeeper to give them the package Mrs. Surratt had delivered, and the guns Herold had stashed there the month before.

After downing whiskey, the two men headed for the home of Dr. Samuel A. Mudd, arriving at 4:00 a.m. Dr. Mudd attended Booth's broken leg, and fed him. The men slept while Mudd had crutches made.

The next afternoon the two fugitives continued their flight to the cabin of Oswell Swan, a Confederate sympathizer. Swan, familiar with the terrain, led the men to their destination the home of Colonel Samuel Cox. Cox ran the Confederate underground between the Maryland and Virginia shores.

Cox secreted the two men in a pine thicket two miles from his house and sent for Thomas Jones, the chief Confederate signal agent in southern Maryland, who ran people across the river to Virginia. While they waited over the next four days for the prowling Federal gunboats to leave, Jones brought the fugitives food, drink and newspapers.

Finally, on April 20, under protection of darkness, Jones led the men from their hiding place to the river -- their last barrier to Virginia. Booth rode a horse while the other two walked a mile to the bluff overlooking the Potomac River. Here Booth dismounted and, with the help of the others, made his way down the slope to the river. Jones drew a small skiff he had hidden in a creek into the shore and motioned the two to get in. With the aid of a compass lit by a candle, the fugitives set out for the Virginia shore two miles distant near Mathias Point.

Booth and Herold didn't make it across the river. Due either to the incoming tide or gunboats, they ended upriver. Instead of crossing to Mathias Point, they landed at Blossom Point on the Maryland side. However, Herold was able to lead them up Maryland's Nanejemoy Creek to the farm of a friend, Peregrin Davis. They hid at the farm until evening, when they again tried to cross.

This time they made it across the Potomac. Following the Virginia shoreline, they arrived at a farm where an operative, William Bryant drove them ten miles to Port Conway. Here they stopped near the ferry slip at the store run by William Rollins. As they waited for the ferry to take them across the Rappahannock River, three Confederate soldiers rode up on their way home. They agreed to accompany the fugitives over the river and help them find refuge. Around noon, the ferry operator took the five men and three horses across to Port Royal.

With men on two of the horses, the party continued two miles to the farm of Richard Garrett. One of the Confederate soldiers, Willie Jett, introduced Booth as James Boyd to the farmer. Garrett, believing Boyd to be a veteran, provided the fugitive with the hospitality of his home. Jett said he would return later and then, with Herold and the other two soldiers, rode twelve miles down the road to Bowling Green.

Then the group split up the next day, with two of the soldiers continuing on their homeward journey. Herold returned to the Garrett farm and Jett, courting the daughter of the innkeeper, stayed on at the Star Hotel.

The day before, as Booth rested peacefully at the farm, a Federal government search party began scouring the nearby countryside questioning people about the whereabouts of the two men.

Working their way southeast, this federal cavalry arrived at Port Conway, Virginia, at noon on April 25. Here they learned that two men answering the description of Booth and Herold had ferried the Rappahannock the day before, together with three Confederate soldiers. Then Bettie Rollins, wife of the store-keeper William Rollins, unwittingly revealed the information the pursuers needed to get their man.

With a woman's interest in romance, she told the cavalry officer that one of the Confederate soldiers was Willie Jett. She added that he undoubtedly had gone to the Star Hotel in Bowling Green to visit his sweetheart.[7]

With that clue, the federal officer in charge figured that if they found Jett, they'd also find Booth.

It was past midnight when the cavalry descended on the Star Hotel. Dropping all formalities, the soldiers dragged the sleeping Jett from his bed and pressed a Army Colt .44 gun to his head. Jett led them to the Garrett farm.

At 2:00 a.m. on April 26, the cavalry troop knocked on the door of the farmhouse. When Garrett, who stuttered when nervous, couldn't answer their question about the men's whereabouts, they put a noose around his neck, threatening to hang him. Just in time, Garrett's son Jack spoke up, telling the officers that the fugitives were in the barn.

The soldiers surrounded the barn and commanded Garrett to unlock the door. They told him to go in and bring out the fugitives.

Herold surrendered. Booth, intending to fight it out with the soldiers, tried to get them to back off so he could come out. To flush him out, the leader of the cavalry ordered the barn torched. As the flames lit the interior, the soldiers saw the figure of a man inside leaning on a single crutch with a carbine in one hand and an Army Colt .44 pistol in the other. As Booth turned toward the barn door, his crutch fell. A shot rang out. The crippled assassin collapsed.

The soldiers carried the mortally wounded but conscious Booth to the porch of the farm house. Hours later -- twelve days after he fired his derringer at Ford's Theater -- Booth died.

With the death of Booth and the capture of Herald, the most sensational manhunt in American history ended. In his eleven day flight, Booth had covered sixty miles. To do so he had needed help. With many Marylanders resenting Lincoln's attempt to keep the state in the Union at all cost -- including imposing virtual martial law -- Booth didn't lack assistance.

Before the government avenged Lincoln's death, eight civilians were also charged with murder. In addition to those from Prince Georges County to Bowling Green, as many as 300 people were hauled in for suspected complicity in the assassination. Only eight were tried, and of these, Dr. Mudd was the only person connected in anyway with the Booth escape.

By the time the military tribunal concluded its trial four would hang and four would go to prison. Mary Surratt was the first woman to be hanged by federal government. Also hanged were conspirators: Herald, Paine and Atzerodt.

***

John Wilkes Booth

John Wilkes Booth's Washington

Ford's Theater, (above) 511 10th Street, N.W. The restored theater where Booth assassinated Lincoln. The downstairs museum displays the five photos of women found in Booth's pocket after his death, the derringer he used to kill Lincoln, the dagger used to stab Major. Henry Rathbone, the date book he used as diary and the compass used during the escape.

Petersen House, 516 10th Street, N.W., across from Ford's Theater. This is the house where Lincoln died in the bed of Booth's actor friend Charles Warwick.

Surratt House, 604 H Street N.W. now an oriental restaurant. A bronze plaque on the outside and historic photo inside acknowledge the site.

Clara Barton
1821-1912

America's Greatest Woman

Born on a farm in Oxford, Massachusetts, Clara Barton rose from obscurity to fame as the leading force behind the establishment of the American Red Cross.

In 1854, Barton moved to Washington and found work as a clerk at the Patent Office. When the Civil War broke out, she supplied food and clothing to soldiers from her hometown when they passed through the capital. By doing so, she learned of the suffering in the field due to lack of supplies. Shortly after, she began soliciting money and supplies through newspaper ads. When these resources poured in, she transported them to sick and wounded soldiers on the frontline.

Four years after the war ended, while recuperating in Europe, the opportunity of her life time knocked at her door. Representatives from the International Red Cross, hearing of her humanitarian concerns, called to ask for her support in getting the United States to join the worldwide organization. Later, upon returning to Washington, she said she would work toward that goal. When a letter arrived naming her as official representative for the International Red Cross, she began the labor that twelve years later would result in her greatest contribution.

With the arrival of the two letters in 1877, she had a mission. After four years of convalescing from a nervous disorder so severe she could not stand alone, Clara Barton arose from her sickbed.

The letter she held from Louis Appia of the International Red Cross, addressed to President Rutherford B. Hayes, established her as the U.S. representative of the international organization. With the letter she determined to convince Congress and the president to authorize America's participation in the humanitarian organization founded six years earlier.

By doing so, America would join a community of nations which agreed on the means for treating wartime wounded. Already thirty-two countries had signed the Geneva Treaty, the agreement which made them part of the International Red Cross. The treaty included a provision that allowed aid to casualties whether they fell in hostile or in friendly territory. Those providing care identified by a red cross symbol -- would be treated as neutrals.

But, as Barton discovered, convincing the legislators and the American public of the value of their country's membership would be difficult. Already the United States had refused three times to sign the Geneva Treaty and thus passed up Red Cross membership. Barton would have to muster all her skill to win this victory.

* * * * *

Barton, although ten years younger than the youngest of her four siblings, joined her brothers in their games. With only boys as playmates, she learned early how to get along with the male of the species -- a skill that benefited her in later life.

When she reached fifteen years of age, her mother, believing her self-confidence needed boosting, urged her to get a job teaching. She got the job and began an eighteen-year-period of teaching which enhanced her sense of responsibility and increased her initiative. When, through her efforts, the Portentous, New Jersey, school where she taught expanded, she played a major part in managing the school. But people didn't like a woman being in charge, so they appointed a male principal. Barton resigned and moved to Washington in 1854.

By the time she arrived in the nation's capital, Barton had matured into young womanhood. About five feet tall, she had an expressive face, and brown eyes. "Her best feature was perhaps a luxuriant growth of glossy hair shading to blackness".[1]   Although not pretty, she walked erect with an air of resolution and strength.

Through a congressman from Massachusetts, Barton was hired as a Patent Office clerk. But she lost that position due to her views on slavery which were counter to President Buchanan's. Thus, when she returned to Washington a second time in 1860 she determined to hold onto her job. To do so, she cultivated the friendship of people in high office and made the right connections. The lessons in military and political strategy that she had learned from her father (an indian fighter and state legislator) assisted her.

By the time the Civil War broke out in 1861, Barton had honed her skills. When President Lincoln called for 75,000 Union volunteers, soldiers packed the capital. Hearing that the Sixth Massachusetts Regiment on their way to Washington from her hometown had been attacked in Baltimore by southern sympathizers, she hurried to the Washington Infirmary to ask if she could help.

She found members of the regiment resting in a makeshift hospital set up in the Senate chamber of the U.S. Capitol. Dozens of wounded men lay suffering from bruises and broken bones. Many had lost their provisions and thus had no food or clothes except those they wore.

Barton set out to nurse and comfort them. To provide them with the food and clothing they needed, she gathered pots, pans and food from her apartment and tore up sheets to make handkerchiefs. She used her own money to buy them summer underwear for the hot days ahead.

Arriving at the Senate with her baskets, she fed the hungry men and then pulled out their hometown paper. Mounting the Speaker's rostrum she read it aloud.[2]

To be sure the Massachusetts Regiment would continue to receive supplies, she ran an advertisement in her hometown newspaper soliciting donations from neighbors and friends. When crates and boxes packed with donations filled her one- room apartment, she got the army quartermaster to warehouse the supplies.

Barton's humanitarian efforts expanded to include others following the first major battle at Bull Run when she found over a thousand wounded men laying on Washington docks, awaiting their turn in the improvised hospital tents. As they waited unbandaged for three to four days for medical attention, the wounded faced the threat of fatal infections or gangrene. Others bled to death.

Noting the dearth of provisions for their care, Barton acted. She cared for as many wounded as possible at her own lodgings and took a leave of absence from her job to nurse others on the docks. She also wrote letters to all her Washington contacts asking for permission to ride onto the battlefields to distribute food and nurse the wounded. When permission arrived from the surgeon general, Barton set out to bring comfort to the wounded at the Second Battle of Bull Run, the Battles of Fairfax Court House, Chantilly, Fredericksburg and Spotsylvania.

Based on the needs she saw, Barton devoted her energy to securing supplies for the relief of their suffering and getting them to the places of greatest need promptly. She worked alone, without the benefit of an organization behind her.

For four years following the war, by this time widely known and respected, Barton was asked to supervise the government's search for missing soldiers and delivered lectures on her war experience.

In 1869, with her health failing, she went abroad to recuperate. It was while she rested at the Geneva home of the family of a soldier she had nursed during the war, that she learned of the International Red Cross. A delegation from that organization, led by Dr. Louis Appia, called on her. Appia, who had heard of Barton's charitable work during the Civil War, assumed she also harbored a broad interest in philanthropy. He asked her why America had not joined the Red Cross and requested her support.

Although the Red Cross was not established until October, 1863, Barton realized how it would have alleviated the suffering of the Civil War and what it might do for her country in the future. She vowed "to take up the question" with her government, as Dr. Appia suggested.[3]

But first, Barton volunteered with the Red Cross when the Franco-Prussian War broke out in 1870. So, it wasn't until seven years later, when she returned to America, that her interest focused on the question of America's participation in the International Red Cross. Fueled by a desire to help victims of the war raging between Russia and Turkey, she sought a way to collect donations. The formation of an American branch of the International Red Cross Society would be the means. To that end she wrote a letter to Appia in Geneva asking permission to promote the Red Cross in America.

* * * * *

In 1877, with the arrival of the letter, Barton's most important work began. With Appia's letter she had her credential since it informed the president of the United States that she had been appointed the official representative of the International Red Cross in America; the letter also asked that the United States sign the Geneva Treaty and thereby become party to it.

As was her way, single-handedly Barton took on the job getting her country to participate. To begin her battle for American membership in the international organization, she assessed the problem: At a time when Americans thought an international body for the care of the wounded unnecessary, she needed to win their acceptance for membership in the International Red Cross. She had to convince a public that believed it would never be involved in a world war that such an organization would be valuable to them.

In essence, Barton had to buck the influence of the Monroe Doctrine's isolationism which dominated most American's thinking. To change people's minds she'd have to capture their imagination. She needed to rally public support before she could get the president's ear. Appia's letter of introduction would not be enough alone.

Also, to prepare for her meeting with the president she had to contact old friends with prominent connections and seek access into the power structure.

When Barton began her campaign, she found to her great surprise that no one knew a thing about the International Red Cross. Thus, her first step in educating both the public and Congress was to write a pamphlet explaining the role of the Red Cross.

As she wrote the pamphlet, she found herself adding an idea that would change everything: the American Red Cross would also offer assistance to peacetime disaster victims. In addition to its work on the battlefield, the Red Cross would rescue ordinary citizens from natural or man-made catastrophes. Although this concept of disaster relief wasn't new, Barton expanded it and put the idea into new perspective.[4]

She then set up a series of lectures and evening soirees, and stopped people she knew in the street to explain the importance of the organization.

Soon Barton had the information she needed to present the case for membership to President Hayes. He listened, expressed interest and referred her to Secretary of State William Evarts. But Evarts wouldn't see her. Through his aide she discovered that the question of America's participation in the International Red Cross had been decided by former Secretary Seward. Barton realized she had the hardest task of all to get the decision reversed.

Determined to succeed, she discussed her proposal with congressmen, some of whom were moved to tears by her stories of suffering soldiers.[5] To gain one senator's support she reminded him that she had saved the life of his brother during Civil War. To win others she appealed to every emotion, including American pride; she pointed out that every civilized nation on earth but the U.S. had signed the treaty and become Red Cross participants. In effect, America was in a class with the barbarians of the world.[6]

Nothing came of her efforts. No Senate resolution made the docket, no official encouraged her. She despaired but she did not do so alone. For although Barton could not legally form the American Red Cross organization without a congressional mandate, she did boast numerous supporters. Even with some interest, however, all official doors were closed. With no idea on how to proceed, in despair, she returned to her home in New York.

When, in September of 1878, a yellow fever epidemic struck inhabitants of the Mississippi Valley. Barton knew what to do. She publicly lamented the refusal of the government to join the International Red Cross. She said that if they had, America would have been in position to organize systematic assistance to the infected region.[7].

With the calamity in people's minds, she returned to Washington to cajole the president and to write to the secretary of state asking for a hearing. But once again the secretary of state refused. Hope flamed when the House of Representatives and the Senate proposed a joint resolution directing President Hayes to sign the Geneva Treaty. The resolution, however, died in committee. Barton returned again to New York.

Eventually as Barton gathered her strength and wrote another letter, this time to the new president, James Garfield. Garfield agreed to receive her and when he did he referred her to the new Secretary of State James G. Blaine.

During the one hour that Blaine kept her waiting, Barton's heart sank; she feared she would again be treated indifferently. She wasn't.

Blaine, ambitious for his country, saw a shift in foreign policy as a means for upgrading America's world role. With his goal of easing the isolationist policy of the Monroe Doctrine, he viewed the Geneva Treaty not as a threat, but as a means of strengthening America's international position.

Telling Barton that both the Senate and war department had to concur in the adoption of the treaty, he recommended she call on the Secretary of War, Robert Lincoln.

During her meeting with Abraham Lincoln's son, Barton reminisced about her meetings with his father and of his great kindness. As she spoke tears spilled down her and Lincoln's cheeks, establishing an emotional tie. Yes, he would support the Red Cross if Blaine recommended it.[8] Barton won similar success with the secretary of the treasury, and congressional leaders. Her optimism grew. Surely, nothing could prevent the treaty being signed now. Or could it?

With membership in the International Red Cross imminent, Barton made plans to establish the organization needed to handle business matters. She gathered her friends and supporters, and wooed them with stories of the horrors of war she had experienced. Then she asked her audience if she should proceed in forming the organization that would be the American Red Cross or step aside. Twenty-two people urged her to pursue the goal and each pledged support as charter members. Among those signing the charter were newspapermen, prominent politicians, long-time personal friends, an author, businessmen and philosophers.

A few weeks later, when President Garfield was shot by a disappointed office seeker, Barton's world collapsed.

With the president hovering between life and death, the question of the treaty was postponed. Even after Chester Arthur was inaugurated, the ratification of the treaty was still uncertain. Would Arthur be in favor?

Without the ratification of the treaty Barton's new organization did not have the congressional charter it needed to begin work. As she waited for action, rival groups vied for control of America's disaster relief.

In September 1881, an opportunity to show how the Red Cross could help came in the form of a Michigan forest fire and drought. The disaster caused the deaths of 500 and extensive property damage. Even without an official organization, Barton asked for donations of clothing, food, and money to aid victims. She also urged people to become members of the pending American Red Cross organization, pointing out that the country needed a reliable organization to distribute donations systematically.

Although her effort produced only moderate success in Michigan, it did point up the need for a permanent organization to improve the relief work. In December 1881 victory came. During his annual message to Congress, President Arthur unconditionally supported passage of the Treaty of Geneva.

Relieved but not ready to sit back, Barton began her two- month campaign with congressmen. She set out systematically to win each senator's support. Using all her diplomatic skills, Barton flattered Senator Elbridge Laphan of New York to sponsor the bill. Next she wooed the Massachusetts congressional delegation with an elegant reception. 7

Because of the Michigan fire relief work conducted by the Red Cross, she knew she had the support of the state's senator. She also gained the support of the press, including Frank Leslie who wrote laudatory editorials and the Associated Press, which sent out frequent dispatches,

At just the moment when Barton was beginning to wonder if she wasn't a crank herself, she received a call from the assistant to the secretary of state. At their meeting, the assistant broke convention by letting Barton see the unsigned treaty. He handed her the soft parchment pages, and asked, "Does it suit you?" With trembling hands, she opened the book and read from beginning to end. "It was a great and solemn document such as she had never before handled; and her life and her hope were bound up in it."[9] Tears streamed down her face.

President Arthur and Secretary Blaine secured confirmation of the treaty by the Senate in March 1882.

After ratification of the treaty, the American Red Cross was officially sanctioned. Barton became its president, a position she held for twenty-three years.

In 1884, Barton was invited by the International Red Cross as the only female delegate to attend the Geneva International Red Cross Conference. She represented the United States at subsequent international conferences in Karlsruhe in 1887, Vienna in 1897 and St. Petersburg in 1902.

For the next two decades she continued to raise money, administer the organization, lecture, write books, and aid disaster victims. Her work took her to Pennsylvania in the wake of the Jonhstown flood, to Russia during the famine of 1892, to Sea Islands, South Carolina, following a hurricane which left 30,000 homeless, and to Turkey following a religious war.

When flooding on the Ohio and Mississippi Rivers left 7000 homeless in 1881 and again in 1884, she chartered a boat and for four months plied the rivers bringing aid to victims. At the end of the Spanish-American War, at age seventy-seven, she stood at the helm of the first relief ship to steam into Cuba's harbor.[10]

For six tumultuous years after her triumphant entry into Cuba in 1898, Barton continued to serve as president of the American Red Cross. Of the growing numbers of chapters, the New York organization, led by an ambitions socialite, Mabel Boardman, dominated as one of the most powerful. With some board members in agreement, Boardman challenged Barton's authority and accused her of misappropriating funds.

In response Barton's supporters replaced the board of directors with people of their own choosing and increased the powers of the president. The rift that this action caused, led to a call for Barton's resignation. After a public investigation, the charges were dropped and Barton's reputation restored. Worn out from the battles within the organization, Barton resigned at age eighty-three.

From the home she had built at Glen Echo, Barton went on to create the National First Aid Society which assisted accident victims. She lived out her last years with her old friend Dr. Julian Hubbell who had been a medical student at the University of Michigan during the Michigan forest fire of 1881. Following their meeting he served the Red Cross as Barton's chief aide for over thirty years.

Until just before her death, passersby reported seeing her at the Glen Echo home she had built, weeding in her garden. Noting the gleaming metal on her chest, the observant saw that the octogenarian wore the medals awarded to her for a lifetime of service.[11] Among them were the Cross of Imperial Russia, Iron Cross of Merit presented by the Emperor of Germany, Gold Cross of Remembrance given to her by the Grand Duke of Baden, and the International Red Cross medal. In addition to these honors, flags from many countries, sent to her in appreciation for her work, brightened the hallways, stairways and gallery rails of her home.

Barton died at her Glen Echo home on April 12, 1912, at age 90. Dr. Hubbell, who was at her bedside, wrote: "She was so much like Christ. She will be in history the greatest of American women if not the greatest in the world."[12]

***

Clara Barton's Washington

Glen Echo Residence, (above) 5801 Oxford Road, off Clara Barton Highway adjacent to Glen Echo Park, Maryland. The house, in the Steamboat Gothic style, is administered by the National Park Service and is open to the public.

Patent Office, now the National Portrait Gallery, 8th & F Streets N.W. where Barton worked in 1854.

American Red Cross Headquarters, 17th & E Streets N.W. where Barton's medals are on exhibit.

Senate Chamber, U.S.Capitol where Barton aided the Sixth Massachusetts Regiment, reading their hometown newspaper to them from the Speaker's rostrum.

Henry Adams
1838-1918

Number Two of Hearts

As great grandson of John Adams and the grandson of John Quincy Adams, Henry Adams carried on a formidable family tradition. Writing about the capital's social and political life, he invented the Washington novel with publication of Democracy *in 1880. He also wrote the nine-volume* History *of the United States, three additional novels, his autobiography (which won the Pulitzer Prize in 1919), biographies, studies and a prodigious correspondence.*

While a professor at Harvard University he met and married a fellow Bostonian, Marion "Clover" Hooper. With their move to Washington in 1877 the home of the witty and urbane couple became the capital's leading social center. Shortly after, Henry and Clover formed with three others an inner circle which they called "The Five of Hearts".

With his friend John Hay, Henry engaged architect H.H. Richardson to build their twin residences. But Clover never set foot in the dream house. Before its completion, tragedy struck.

Returning to his wife Clover's bedroom on that Sunday morning shortly before Christmas of 1885, Henry Adams intended to stay only long enough to tell her that a caller waited downstairs. Instead, he ran to his wife and fell to his knees.

Clover lay crumpled on the rug in front of the fireplace. Beside her an open phial poured out the remainder of its contents: potassium cyanide. The unmistakable odor of the chemical she used in developing her photographic plates filled the room.

Thinking she had fainted, Henry dragged his wife to the sofa and lifted her onto it. Then he ran to the residence of his neighbor, Doctor Charles Hagner. The two returned to the room where the fire still burned in the fireplace. Clover remained motionless. The doctor bent over the lifeless woman. "Dead", he pronounced. After drinking the poisonous chemical, Clover's heart had stopped beating. She had died almost instantly.[1]

Henry told his neighbor not to let anyone come near him. When a friend came to his door, he sent him away. He sent a telegram via a servant to Clover's family and to his brother. Then he sat by the window and waited.

When the family members gathered the next day for an evening meal, Henry wore a red tie. Refusing to mourn, he tore off the black crepe from his arm and threw it under the table. Six days later he assured his friends that the only chance of saving what was left of his life rested on his "going straight ahead without looking behind".

"Never fear for me," he wrote to a friend. "I have had happiness enough to carry me over some years of misery .... I admit that fate at last has smashed the life out of me; for twelve years I had everything I most wanted on earth ... as long as any will is left, I shall try not to complain."[2]

Henry moved into his new house, and settled down to his routine life and work; he read Shakespeare at night, and went for walks. He wrote to a friend that he tried "to think of nothing but how to make the days pass till my nerves get steady again".[3]

Why did she commit suicide? Some said that Clover, a restless spirit, always wanted more than she had. Others suggested that from the time they were married Clover's bouts with depression hinted at her final act; even during her honeymoon she had suffered a nervous breakdown.

Most believed the obvious: her death was caused by the severe depression that had plagued her since her father's death nine months earlier. Extremely attached to her father, she had relied on him since her mother's death when Clover was five-years-old. For thirteen years, Clover wrote to her father every Sunday, depending on him to hear her thoughts. She listened to his voice in those letters. When he died of angina, Clover acknowledged that she was "utterly crushed. Nothing in her life seemed any longer to have any meaning."[4]

Henry loved Clara. "I am absurdly in love." he wrote to his brother.[5] Clara wrote to her sister that Henry "is more patient and loving than words can express."[6] But Henry's love could not save Clover.

Clover and Henry met in London. Henry, who called himself a "social butterfly", had broken into the whirl of London society; he even had been presented to Queen Victoria.[7] Clover, a native of Boston, stopped in London following her travels on the continent. As fellow Bostonians they were introduced at the American legation.

When the prospect of a position in the history department at Harvard University called, Henry returned to Boston. Pursuing his study of history, Henry found himself twice a week in the home of Clover's brother-in-law, Professor Gurney. At the same time, Clover began to study Greek with Gurney. It was only a matter of time until the two met again, renewing their London acquaintance.

Soon after their meeting, Henry wrote to his brother Charles that he found Clover "superior to any woman he had ever met ... even though she has a certain vein of personality which approaches eccentricity. This is very attractive to me, but then I am absurdly in love .... I do not think it worthwhile to resist... the fascination of a clever woman who chooses to be loved." Henry threw himself "head over heels into the pursuit."[8]

Charles disapproved, saying the Hooper family were all "crazy as coots" and that Clover would "kill herself just like her aunt". To make his point, Charles had pointed to Clover's aunt who took arsenic while pregnant with her second child at age 28.[9]

Nevertheless, in 1872 Henry married Clover in a small ceremony at her family home. Immediately after, the two began a one-year honeymoon, visiting London, Dresden, Berlin, Venice, Naples, Paris and voyaging up the Nile for three months. Together they shopped for furniture for the house they would one day acquire.

Returning to Boston, the couple lived there for five years until Henry gave up his professorship and they moved to Washington. While a young man Henry had worked in the capital as a newspaper correspondent and retained "a passionate sense that he belonged there, if not as a politician, then as an observer of politicians." [10]

Instead of playing an active role in politics as had his ancestors, Henry decided to write about leaders and power. He began by editing the papers of Albert Gallatin, Thomas Jefferson's secretary of the treasury and later his minister to Britain.

The Adams rented the home of William W. Corcoran (the art gallery founder) one block from Lafayette Square. The couple settled into the life of social Washington. Their home, filled with art treasures and rare carpets purchased during their overseas trips, became "the Little White House". Each day at five o'clock exclusive society gathered for tea: the president of the United States, congressmen, the Supreme Court justices, famous authors, actors, and explorers.

Within this rarefied atmosphere arose an even more exclusive group: an inner-circle named "The Five of Hearts". With their three friends, biographer John Hay, Clara Hay, and explorer Clarence King, they exchanged confidences on specially-printed notepaper that depicted playing cards. At their secret meetings, the quintet gossiped, noting in their minutes the most scandalous events of the day.

With their friends and position, Clover and Henry seemed the ideal couple. They took long walks through the wilderness along the Potomac River and woods behind Georgetown. They rode, she on her mare Daisy and he astride his horse Prince. As Henry wrote after Clover's death, "for twelve years I had everything I most wanted on earth."[11]

With the anonymous publication of Henry's novel *Democracy*, people speculated about the author of the merciless depiction of Capital life. Some thought Clover had written the shocking expose, others suspected Henry.

As Lafayette Square neighbors wondered at the mysterious author of the book, Henry and John Hay decided to build adjoining residences on Lafayette Square. They hired the leading architect of the day, Henry Hobson Richardson.

About this time, Clover began pursuing a new hobby, photography, inspired by the Civil War photos by Mathew Brady she had purchased. She bought a camera and took photos of such upper-class luminaries as Abigail Adams and Jerome Bonaparte. In the darkroom she had set up, Clover used a number of chemicals including potassium cyanide to develop her plates.

Though he tried to blame Clover's death on factors outside of his control, guilt ravaged Henry. Voices whispered that no one -- not even the most despondent commits suicide without cause.[12]

Henry saw only one answer to his grief and loneliness: flight. With his friend John LaFarge he traveled to Japan. Although the visit provided little comfort, it gave him the idea for a monument to Clover. Visiting the Imperial Tombs at Nikko, Henry saw a statue of the goddess Kwannon. To him the statue's serene face spoke of timeless contemplation. As such, it seemed the perfect expression for his wife's memorial.

Upon returning to Washington, Henry commissioned sculptor Augustus Saint-Gaudens to create a bronze figure to mark Clover's Rock Creek Cemetery grave. He gave no hint other than to say he wanted the figure to symbolize "the acceptance, intellectually, of the inevitable". He also specified that the memorial bear neither her name nor any inscription. For Henry, the anonymous memorial should symbolize "all the meaning we know and cannot grasp, all the suffering wonder in us that is never satisfied, all the need in us that ends in peace without emptiness and, finally, in emptiness without terror."[13]

After Henry agreed to one of the poses and paid Saint-Gaudens $20,000 for the monument, he closed further discussion. "I don't want to see the statue until it's finished."[14] Henry refused to communicate further on the project, using as his reason that he wanted Saint-Gaudens to be free to proceed without interference. The sculptor begged his patron to come see and approve the clay model of the proposed statue. Henry did not respond.

Saint-Gaudens sculpted his interpretation of Kwannon from the photographs of the statue that Henry had given him. Although the face of the Japanese goddess looked nothing like lively but plain Clover Adams, then, as now, it expressed something of the mystery surrounding Clover's life and death.

Upon completion of the memorial, the artist installed the six-foot high bronze figure, a woman enveloped in a shroud. He had revealed only her forearm, hand, and face with its downcast eyes. The brooding statue, set in a curve of holly trees, marked the lonely grave silently; no etched words hinted at the tragedy that the figure represented.

When, at last, Henry viewed Saint-Gaudens' work he was impressed. He later wrote that "every detail interested him: every line; every touch of the artist's, every change of light and shade, every point of relation."[15]

Just as the motive for Clover's suicide isn't clear, so the figure guarding her grave conjures mystery. Some people see the figure as an expression of melancholy and despair. Mark Twain gave it the name it now bears: "Grief". Henry, on the other hand, saw no interpretation but the obvious -- his own: "the figure expressed the peace of God ... the oldest idea known to human thought."[16]

Henry lived another thirty-three years after Clover's death. He completed the last three of his nine-volume *History of the United States.* Its publication in 1891 placed Adams in the first rank among American historians.

With the history completed, Henry sought rest and recreation in travel. Spending part of each year at his house in Washington, he traveled with his friend LaFarge and on his own for four years visiting Hawaii, Tahiti, Cuba, Yellowstone, Europe, Russia, Sweden, Egypt and Paris.

Although this was the most unproductive period in his life, it prepared Henry for writing the two works for which he will be remembered longest. One, *Mont-Saint-Michel and Chartres*, interprets medieval life and philosophy. The second, *The Education of Henry Adams*, contributes to the philosophy of history in its study of the multiplicity of early twentieth-century life.[17]

After his friends Hay and King died, Henry in 1905 wrote that it was time for him to go. He lived another fourteen years and continued to write until his nerves were badly shaken upon hearing about the sinking of the *Titanic* -- the vessel on which he had planned to sail to Europe. Even with impaired vision resulting from that shock, he continued his intellectual pursuits by studying medieval songs and writing letters.

Shortly before his passing at age eighty, Henry wrote of his wife in a letter grieving the death of their friend Henry James: "I have clung to all that belonged to my wife. I have been living all day in the seventies [the 1870's when they resided in Washington] ... indeed, we really were happy then."[18]

Henry Adams

In his autobiography, published after his death, Adams wrote that he and Hay looked out the windows of their residences on Lafayette Square "with a sense of having all that anyone had; all that the world had to offer; all that they wanted in life."

***

Henry Adam's Washington

Rock Creek Cemetery, off North Capitol Street at Rock Creek Church Road & Webster Street, N.W. Grave of Clover Adams marked by famous Saint-Gaudens sculpture (above). Henry lies buried beside her.

Adams Residence, once his residence stood on the site of Hay-Adams Hotel, 16th & H Streets N.W. The ground floor arches of the famous structure, built by architect Henry Hobson Richardson, are reinstalled at the garage entrance at 2618 31st Street N.W.

John Philip Sousa

1854-1932

He Played To Their Hearts

John Philip Sousa, bandmaster and composer, earned the world's exuberant applause. By age forty, after serving over half his lifetime in the U.S. Marine Band, he formed his own concert band. Almost overnight, the Sousa Band became the most successful in the nation.

He and his band toured the United States and Europe giving over 10,000 concerts. By the time he gave up the baton almost forty years later, Sousa, "The March King" reigned as the best known musician in the world.

Composer of over a hundred marches and a genial and handsome bandmaster, Sousa became to the march what the Viennese Johann Strauss was to the waltz.[1]

Born in Washington, Sousa began his musical education at age six. From childhood he was passionately fond of music and wanted to be a musician.[2] *By the time he was thirteen the young Sousa had organized a small orchestra, and played his violin like a professional.*

On a June night in 1868, thirteen-year-old John Philip Sousa dreamed of beautiful ladies in spangled tights and of buckets filled with pink lemonade.[3] On waking he felt a thrill of excitement, realizing his dream would soon come true. Because, that very evening, he would join the circus as the crew struck tents in Washington and headed to the next town. He would run away with the circus to a life of wonder and excitement.

Sousa had made that decision suddenly. Just the day before, a man from the circus, knocked on his door, and explained that he had heard Sousa playing his fiddle from the street. He introduced himself as the circus band master and declared he had a place for Sousa to play his fiddle. "Have you ever thought of joining a circus?"

The talented young Sousa admitted that no, indeed, he had never thought of the circus as his career. But, "Yes, it's a wonderful idea." Sousa's thoughts raced. "I can follow the life of the circus, make money and become the leader of a circus band myself!"[4]

The idea of a career as a musician wasn't new. After all, Sousa's father and brother both played brass instruments in the U.S. Marine Band. Over six years before he had made up his mind to play in a band, too. Enrolled in a music academy since that decision, he already played the violin like a professional as well as a variety of brass instruments too.

"Yes, I'd like to join the circus," he said responding to the band director. "But," he hesitated, "I don't think my father will let me go." John Philip explained that since his father was "so nice" he wouldn't think of leaving without asking him and "No, I don't think he'll let me go".

The bandmaster conceded that Sousa's father might forbid him from coming. But that's because fathers don't "understand the future for a boy traveling with a circus. Come with us," he urged. "After a day or two write your father and tell him what a good time you are having. That way he probably won't interfere."[5]

Overcome with the promise of a life of playing music and of adventure, Sousa agreed to keep his plans a secret from his father and to report to the circus the following evening. Bursting with excitement, he had to tell someone. Since he couldn't tell his father, Sousa reasoned that he'd tell his playmate Edward. What harm could that do?

Edward listened, his eyes growing wider as Sousa described his future circus triumphs. "There I'll be," he said, looking at the pictures in his mind, "I'll conduct a gigantic band beneath a monster tent that reaches upwards to the stars."[6]

But the circus tent and band which had been so oversized in Sousa's imagination one day, shrank to nothing the next. On the day which was to have begun the great adventure, Sousa awoke to his father's gentle voice saying, "Good morning, Son. When you dress today, put on your Sunday clothes."[7]

All through breakfast Sousa wondered why he had to wear his Sunday clothes on a weekday. After breakfast, his father asked his son to walk with him to the Marine Barracks, several blocks from their home. Passing through the entrance gate, Sousa saw once again the grand old house where the commandant of the Marine Corps lived. Turning from it, walking beside his father, Sousa crossed the parade grounds to the office of the commandant of the Marine Band.[8]

The record of the Marine Corps says that John Philip Sousa enlisted on the 9th day of June 1868 with the permission of his father Antonio Sousa.

Sousa gradually discovered what had happened. News of his exciting plans had gotten out. The secret he had told Edward traveled quickly from his playmate, to Edward's mother, and finally to his father.

Instead of confronting John Philip, his father simply made other plans with his friend, Marine Band Commandant General Zeilin. To a protective father there was only one solution. As other young boys had, Sousa would be enlisted in the Marine Band as an apprentice to study music until he got over his infatuation with the circus. Although no ladies in spangled tights would perform as Sousa played, at least the young dreamer would play in a band.

Sousa loved band music for two reasons: his father played trombone with the Marine Band and, like all young boys, he thrilled to the sound. As far back as he could remember, his heart beat faster whenever he heard the beating drums and blaring brass instruments of the military bands parading up and down Pennsylvania Avenue. During the Civil War years almost all of the U.S.Army military units sponsored their own bands. Bands were so popular, in fact, that to stop their proliferation, congress had issued a moratorium to prevent new ones from forming.

For Sousa, most memorable had been the bands accompanying the marching feet of the victorious Union soldiers parading down Pennsylvania Avenue at the end of the war. "Tramp, Tramp, Tramp The Boys Are Marching" the music still resounded in Sousa's ears. "Plunk, plunk, plunk, the boys are marching' till yer couldn't rest," he wrote.[9]

As a member of the Marine Band, the corps' top marching unit, Sousa would play that same rousing music. The band, which was established in 1801 by Thomas Jefferson as "The President's Own" would perform at official functions including those at the White House for the president.

From his beginnings as a band boy, Sousa marched and played for seven years. Then he resigned after five years to study violin, harmony and theory. Invited to rejoin as band director, Sousa returned to the group in 1880. For the next twelve years he led the band, playing for five presidents and audiences that grew larger and larger..

As director of the Marine Band, Sousa turned what had been a lackluster group into one the nation's most popular musical bands. The improvements came about because Sousa believed that music should please the listener. To the delight of his audiences he got rid of the limited repertoire from which previous band leaders had drawn. In place of selections from old Italian operas, uninteresting overtures and ordinary marches and polkas, he substituted light opera, marches, polkas, and other lively pieces. He devised instrumentation for the horns that allowed effects as soft as those in a symphony orchestra. Within his first year as director he introduced six marches of his own, and continued adding new ones throughout his twelve years of leadership.

Sousa also elevated the band to national eminence by weeding out the band's weak musicians; he made rehearsals exceptionally strict with long hours and hard work. He then replaced those who resigned with the best musicians of his acquaintance.

People responded to the improvements by flocking to the concerts. The band was in demand at the White House, playing for presidents including the wedding of President Cleveland. Sousa's fame grew and the successful band master had a new dream. He would form a group of his own and tour the world.

In 1892, he realized that dream. He brought together the finest musicians in America and for the next thirty-nine years he and his Sousa New Marine Band traveled the globe. The band's first important engagement was the 1893 World's Columbian Exposition, in Chicago.

Following that success, Sousa and his men went on to cover over one million miles giving ten thousand concerts throughout the United States and in Europe. They traveled by train to cities and also to small towns. Over the years as people in hundreds of small towns heard the Sousa band play its fame spread.

Sousa's band became famous because its director combined in his program serious classical compositions (which he rearranged) with popular tunes and his rousing marches. "He demonstrated that a concert band could play most classical selections as well as a symphony orchestra."[10]

To this program he added a flair for showmanship; he dressed impeccably, used dramatic touches where he could, and hired the best public relations man available to promote the band. By doing so, he made people feel they weren't just hearing a concert but participating in an important event.

"His name was magic ... When his band came to town other activities ceased". Businessmen closed their doors, teachers dismissed their students, Flags were hoisted.

Sousa had captured the heart of the nation and laid to rest the long-held European prejudice against American music. "Before his time, there existed a strange but highly effective prejudice against American names in music. American composers and performers had to have European names to be accepted by the American public".[11]

By the time he died, Sousa reigned as the best known musician in the world. People called him "The March King". He achieved the status of royalty because his music played to people's hearts.

Besides being appreciated as a performer, John Philip Sousa was equally famous as a composer. In his lifetime he composed 16 operettas, 36 marches, 11 suites, 23 dances, and 70 songs; he wrote 9 books and 132 articles.

Although he never got to follow his boyhood dream of playing under the big top, Sousa's arena competed with "the biggest show on earth". He performed on the greatest stages of the world. Honors and decorations were showered on him: the Royal Victorian Order of Great Britain, the Golden Palms and Rosette of the French Academy, and the Cross of

Artistic Merit of the Academy of Arts, Sciences and Literature of Hainault, Belgium.

Famous, wealthy, surrounded by thrilling music he created, and much loved, Sousa lived the life he had dreamed. At the end of his life, speaking of the inevitable time when "I shall lay down my baton, " he said he would call back "the melodies of a thousand happy concerts, re-awakened the echoes of many a stirring march and tuneful opera. If, out of the cadences of time, I have evoked one note that, clear and true, vibrates gratefully on the heartstrings of my public -- I am well content."[12]

***

John Philip Sousa's Washington

John Philip Sousa

Marine Barracks, 8th & I Streets S.E. where he practiced and paraded. He saw the Commandant's House (above), built in 1805, as he crossed the parade grounds with his father to the Marine Band commandant's office on the day of his enlistment.

Family Residence, 318 Independence Avenue S.E. where he lived until he was married.

Sousa Bridge, Pennsylvania Avenue's northwestern extension crosses the Anacostia River on this bridge named after him.

Christ Church Capitol Hill, 620 G St. S.E. the 1807 church, on the National Register of Historic Places, stands three doors east of his home. He and his family were members.

Congressional Cemetery, 18th & E Streets, S.E. A small but exquisitely proportioned Greek structure marks his grave.

World War I Memorial, Reflecting Pool grounds, where he played at the Armistice Day 1931 dedication.

Evalyn Walsh McLean

1886-1947

The Diamond's Curse

Socialite and hostess, Evalyn Walsh McLean epitomizes the opulent lifestyle of Washington's Gilded Age. Born in Denver, her world changed when her father struck it rich in a Colorado gold mine. Moving to Washington in 1898, the Walsh family built a 64-room mansion where they entertained diplomats and kings.

After her marriage to wealthy Cincinnati newspaper scion Edward B. McLean, Evalyn entertained Washington aristocracy and Republican leaders at their northwest Washington estate. In the 1930's a newspaper column she wrote, for the Washington Star and her lavish parties for a hundred guests, turned her into a celebrity.

But of all that testifies to Evalyn's glamorous life, none holds more fascination than her 42-carat Hope diamond. When she purchased the stone she knew it carried a curse. She rejected the thought that the curse would affect her life.

*T*he last time she had seen the jewel it shimmered at the throat of a sultan's harem favorite. Now, as Pierre Cartier broke the wax seal and stripped away the wrappings, Evalyn Walsh McLean touched the Hope diamond.

Evalyn had never seen a diamond this shade of blue. It was too dark to be the blue of Chinese ceramics, too gray to be the pale blue of West Point uniforms. Was the blue a shade like delft or more like the blue of tropical water? She felt that nature had been torn between forming a diamond or a sapphire, resulting in a gem that was some of each.

* * * * *

Evalyn knew a great deal about diamonds. Her jewel boxes overflowed with the gems including the Star of India a 32- grain pearl set in triple loops of diamonds. As the daughter of Thomas Walsh, Evalyn had lived in diamond-studded opulence from the day in 1896 when her father struck it rich in a Colorado gold mine.

Shortly before Walsh could verify his find, Evalyn's mother had noted, when he came home late one night, that his eyes were so bright she thought he had a temperature. Although he suffered from jaundice, this time the feverish look was caused by the gleam of gold his prospecting pick had uncovered.

Evalyn found out first. With her mother away in Denver nursing her own ailing mother, Evalyn's father needed someone else with whom he could share his secret. And as a sick man, Thomas knew that if he were to die, his discovery would perish with him.

He called ten-year-old Evalyn to his bedroom. Motioning Evalyn to come around the side of his bed, he showed her a piece of grayish quartz. With his tongue he wet the rock and held it near Evalyn's eyes. The specks of gold glistened. "Daughter, I've struck it rich," he whispered.[1]

Born into a poor Irish peasant family, Walsh ended up talking with presidents and kings. At the 64-room mansion he built on Washington's Embassy Row at 2020 Massachusetts Avenue, the Walshes entertained with unmatched lavishness.

Evalyn Walsh McLean

To celebrate the completion of their $850,000 palace in 1903, the Walsh family staged what the *Washington Star* newspaper called the greatest party of the century. The gold brocade walls matched the gold damask table linens strewn with gold orchids. The serving pieces gleamed; they were made of gold nuggets from the Camp Bird mine![2]

Five years after the opening of the Walsh mansion, Evalyn married wealthy Edward B. McLean, son of the publisher of the *Cincinnati Inquirer*. The two met at the 1908 Democratic Convention in Denver on which he was reporting for his father's paper.

During their honeymoon in Paris, Evalyn bought the Star of the East, a 92-carat emerald. During their visit to Turkey in 1908 she saw the Hope diamond for the first time. Evalyn could not forget the gem.

* * * * *

Now, as jeweler Pierre Cartier placed the Hope diamond in her hands in 1922, Evalyn listened to the legend of the gem's curse. Cartier told her that it's most recent victim had been the harem favorite Evalyn had seen wearing the huge blue diamond in Turkey; after the sultan had been dethroned, she was stabbed to death.

Prior to that, others who owned the diamond had died violently. First, a French adventurer named Tavernier who smuggled the gem from India to the court of Louis XIV, was torn and eaten by wild dogs. Tavernier had stolen the gem that served as the eye of a Hindu idol.

The French king and his queen, Marie Antoinette, who added the diamond to their crown jewels, suffered the stone's curse when they climbed to the guillotine and had their heads chopped off during the French Revolution. Following their death, the French revolutionaries seized the royal jewels; among the gems inventoried was the diamond. But shortly after the revolution, the diamond disappeared.

In 1830, it turned up in London, where a diamond dealer sold the blue stone to London banker Henry Thomas Hope. The banker gave the diamond to his daughter. She willed it to her son who married a music-hall actress named Mae Yohe, who wore the jewel on stage.

Then the diamond disappeared once again. Years later an old jewel dealer who sold jewels he found in pawn shops and second-hand stores, appeared at the door of the London jeweler who had sold the diamond to Hope years before. From his bag the dealer dumped a collection of dirty gems he had bought at a sheriff's sale. The jewels the trader displayed where among the effects of a music hall actress named Mae Yohe. She had disappeared from her boarding house without paying the rent. Only the trader knew the jewels where not the shoddy imitations the landlady and others believed them to be.

The jeweler, recognizing the Hope diamond among the hoard, advised the trader to contact the trustees of the Hope estate. He did, surrendered the collection and received a fair reward.

According to legend, the gem next traveled to Catherine the Great of Russia. Catherine died of apoplexy. Its next owner sold the diamond just before his ship sunk and he was drowned.

At the beginning of the 20th century, a merchant sold the diamond to the Turkish sultan. He didn't live long enough to spend his earnings from the sale; he, his wife and children died when their car dove off a cliff.

From the Turkish harem where Evalyn saw it in 1905, the gem turned up years later in Paris where Cartier bought it from a man named Rosenau.

Because of its distinctive color, Evalyn was convinced it had once glittered in the crown of the French king. But as for the stories about the tragedies befalling the diamond's owners, Evalyn scoffed. "For me, bad luck objects are lucky charms," she said. But when Evalyn took the gem home on a trial basis as Cartier suggested, she soon gave the diamond to her husband, asking him to return it to Cartier. "I don't like the setting," she explained.[3]

Cartier, who had sold her so many baubles in the past, persisted. He changed the diamond's setting, framing the blue diamond in a necklace of white diamonds. Then he sent it back for Evalyn with the request that she keep it for a few days.

It took less than a day for Evalyn to make her decision. "For hours the jewel stared at me ....", she wrote, "At some time during the night I began to want the thing."[4]

What of the curse? Evalyn who at first rejected the idea and felt she knew better, did admit to believing in a number of superstitions. Included among these, she eventually admitted, was the curse of the Hope diamond. Because of this, she vowed she would never let her children or friends touch it. She herself, however, was immune to evil.

She bought the bauble for $154,000. When her mother discovered this she lectured Evalyn, saying the cursed stone must be sent back. Evalyn refused, arguing that everybody has bad luck. More warnings came. Every day letters told her of the diamond's curse, some implored her to sell it. One came from former owner Mae Yohe who blamed the diamond for her ruin. She begged Evalyn to throw it away and break the spell. With each letter, Evalyn felt a thrill, "as if a curtain was about to rise on a play -- her life."[5]

Although thrilled, Evalyn admitted she was nervous.

To ally her fears she decided to try to "foil the devil" of the gem. She went to her priest and asked him to bless it for her. The priest agreed, placing the jewel on a velvet cushion. No sooner had he donned his robe and begun the procedure than a storm broke. Although no wind blew or rain fell, the darkened sky turned lurid. Lighting flashed at the windows.

From that day forward Evalyn wore the diamond as a charm, averring it brought her good luck. She wrote: "There are those who would believe that somehow a curse is housed deep in the blue of the Hope diamond. I scoff at that in the privacy of my mind, for I do comprehend the source of what is evil in our lives ... the natural consequences of unearned wealth in undisciplined hands."[6]

No matter what the cause, luck seemed to run out for Evalyn.

Upon return to Washington from their honeymoon, the McLeans had built a country estate on upper Wisconsin Avenue which they named Friendship. Maintained by a staff of thirty, the lavish 80-acre estate boasted gardens, greenhouses with $50,000 worth of roses, a duck pond, stables and a golf course. Here they entertained the rich and famous: ambassadors, congressmen, presidents and leaders of industry.

One year after their marriage, Evalyn bore their first child Vinnie. Newspaper headlines called him "the hundred million dollar baby," because of the empire he would one day inherit.[7] Evalyn considered that figure an understatement, considering his prospects as an heir.

Evalyn felt for the child an unbounded love. Vinnie lay in a golden crib, a gift from King Leopold of Belgium. His clothes came from Europe's Worth, the most expensive designer in Paris. To warm him on his carriage rides he wore a hat and coat made of ermine; a robe of the same fur lay over his legs.

No luxury was spared the young heir. Because of Evalyn's fear of kidnapping, Vinnie was guarded by a staff and had six automobiles assigned to him. He was always driven by a chauffeur so that he avoided the risk of accident or contamination that might result from using public transport. Rather than going to the circus, the performers came to Vinnie and put on a private show. The year after his mother purchased the Hope diamond, his Christmas present included a $40,000 working model of the Panama Canal locks and a miniature steam yacht.

But money could not buy one thing: When Vinnie was nine years old he was struck by an automobile. The child had playfully snatched ferns off the gardeners truck. Attempting to dodge the gardener, who pursued him, Vinnie suddenly changed directions in the street. The Tin Lizzie approaching at a slow pace barely touched the child. Vinnie fell but immediately got up and walked back to his house. He seemed all right. Doctors said he had not fractured his skull. Within hours, however, the boy was paralyzed and shortly after died.

The tragedies continued. Evalyn's mother-in-law, one of the first to touch the gem, died within a year. Her father in- law-died prematurely of a heart attack.

Ned began drinking heavily. Their marriage floundered and the couple separated in 1928. Ned was confined to a mental institution where he died in 1941.

Following these tragedies, Evalyn tried to overcome her grief. She began writing a daily column for the *Washington Times* and continued giving her lavish parties. With the outbreak of World War II, her parties continued but instead of hosting society, she invited enlisted personnel and hospital workers to her Georgetown mansion. At these parties she would don all of her jewels and, taking off a ring, bracelet, necklace or brooch, give it to a guest to wear for the evening. One day she gave the Hope diamond to a veteran in a wheelchair; he wore it on his cast. At other times she amused her guests by fastening the gem around the head of her dog, which then ran free in the house sporting her bauble.

In 1946 tragedy again struck. Her twenty-five-year-old daughter Evalyn Reynolds who had married a flamboyant senator, overdosed on sleeping pills and died. A year later, Evalyn broke her hip and while convalescing contracted pneumonia. After much suffering she died in that year.

In the settlement of Evalyn's estate, her jewels were sold to New York gem merchant Harry Winston. For under $1 million Winston bought the

Hope diamond, a 20-pound gold nugget her father had cast as a souvenir of his mining days, and the Star of India. Although he didn't believe in the curse of the Hope diamond, he didn't want his wife wearing it. So Winston gave the jewel to the Smithsonian Institution.

Today the gem reigns behind thick glass at the National Museum of Natural History. Since the stone is now owned by the Federally-funded institution, some wonder if its spell hasn't been cast on the United States government.

***

Evalyn Walsh McLean's Washington

Walsh Mansion, (above) 2020 Massachusetts Avenue, N.W. now the Indonesian Embassy.

Hope diamond, the jewel gleams at the Smithsonian Institution's Natural History Museum.

Friendship, on a site at Wisconsin Avenue near R Street N.W., once reigned Evalyn's estate with its golf course, stables and greenhouses.

Rock Creek Cemetery, north of Rock Creek Road & Upshur Street N.W., she is buried in the McLean family vault.

Alice Roosevelt Longworth
1884-1977

Outrageous Alice

The beautiful and outrageous daughter of Teddy Roosevelt rose to near royalty status when her father became president in 1901. Alice's pranks and disregard for social conventions entertained readers across America as the media watched her every move.

A fascination with politics dominated her life. She advised her presidential father, campaigned for her congressman husband, and befriended political greats. In a remarkable and long life her outspoken commentary on politics and politicians enlivened Washington.

Alice, born in Albany, New York, was brought up by her aunt as her mother died giving birth to her. Alice came to Washington after her father was elected president and lived with him and his second wife in the White House. Wild and headstrong, Alice caused her father to respond when he was asked why he didn't control her: "I can be president of the United States, or I can attend to Alice".

*I*n the fall of 1905, front page stories speculated on rumors that the president's daughter was engaged. As a result of this gossip, Alice felt pushed into a corner; if she didn't confess the truth, screaming headlines would. But first, she'd have to get her parents' blessing. Without that there could be no White House wedding and she'd miss the opportunity to outshine her rivals by staging the wedding of the century.

So, with the pressure building, after four weeks of procrastinating, Alice anxiously approached her stepmother Edith Carow. She waited until Edith had a toothbrush in her mouth, busily brushing. By announcing her engagement when her stepmother could not immediately respond, Alice hoped to give her a moment to think before she spoke disparagingly of her fiancee, Nick Longworth.[1]

Meanwhile Nick was asking Alice's father, the president of the United States, for his daughter's hand. As Nick spoke, Theodore Roosevelt responded favorably. He liked Nick's family ties, his political aspirations, and the fact that he, like himself, held membership in Harvard University's prestigious Porcellian Club.[2]

Since the president closed his ears to any talk that bordered on the salacious, news of Nick's womanizing had not reached him. But even if he had known the worst, he might have given Nick Alice's hand.

On that day in 1905 both Alice and Nick waited nervously for the answer to their question. Would the couple receive the blessing of the Roosevelts and thereby have the chance to make history by marching down the aisle in the White House East Room?

* * * * *

More a tomboy than a femme fatal, Alice nevertheless boasted a beautiful face and a regal carriage. Her hair was "an indefinite blonde"; her eyes were "queer, attractive long shape, a phosphorescent grayish blue, changing color according to her moods."[3]

With only a small inheritance from the Roosevelts in the offing, Alice needed a husband with a comfortable income. Because she sought the spotlight, she also needed a man who had enough self-esteem to stand in the shadows.

The president realized that the man who married Alice would take on a full-time job. Roosevelt's experience had told him that managing his rambunctious daughter wasn't easy. When asked why he didn't do a better job of controlling her, Roosevelt summed up the magnitude of the problem with his response: "I can be president of the United States or I can attend to Alice."[4]

Alice's behavior grew out of her insatiable desire for attention. After her mother died hours after bearing her, Roosevelt put his sister Anne in charge of baby Alice. Pretty much ignored by her father, Alice lived with her aunt most of her young life. Even after Roosevelt remarried three years after her mother's death, Alice spent only a brief time in her father and stepmother's home.

To compensate for this lack of parental attention, Alice craved the spotlight. She smoked, drank, got tickets for speeding, and bet on horses. When her father ascended to the presidency in 1901, Alice's exploits became front page news. The more outrageous her pranks the more the appetite of the press grew. With his daughter in the headlines, Roosevelt was often furious. He ordered her to behave. She refused.

She cared only about amusing herself. With that goal guiding her she shocked guests by eating asparagus at a White House dinner without removing her gloves. Unchaperoned, she drove her car around Washington and was stopped for speeding. She appeared on a railroad platform with a boa constrictor wrapped around her neck. She jumped into a swimming pool dressed in a white linen suit. When her father told her she couldn't smoke under the White House roof, she climbed on top of the roof to puff her cigarettes.[5]

With her father constantly criticizing her behavior, Alice at age twenty-one she "had to get away from the White House" as soon as possible.[6] Her eagerness increased when she got the announcement that her cousin Eleanor was to marry Franklin Roosevelt. Alice took a dim view of her father's offer to host that wedding in the White House. She vowed she would be the first White House bride of her generation.

So, when at about this time Alice met tall, handsome, thirty- six-year-old Nick Longworth, she set her cap for him.[7] The wealthy young man had just arrived in Washington to serve his first term as representative from Cincinnati. Nick, whose father had made a fortune in real estate, chose politics as an amusing pastime. Such a career allowed him plenty of time to indulge in his true passions: playing the violin, drinking wine, and pursuing women.

Rather than taking Alice out alone, he escorted her and her friend. the Russian ambassador's daughter Countess Margarite (Maggie) Cassini, to his club for dinner. The threesome became a sensation. Soon newspapers began reporting that he couldn't make up his mind between the two. People made bets on which woman he'd marry.

Maggie didn't know for a long time that Alice had fallen in love with Nick, but she did note that Alice was happiest when Nick was around.[8] Maggie also found Nick attractive and flirted outrageously with him. Nick fell for Maggie and proposed. When he asked Maggie to marry him, they were sledding back from Chevy Chase to Washington. Getting out to fix a broken harness, Nick said "this is the last time I'll ask". With that Maggie grabbed the reigns, flicked the whip, and left him standing in the snow. "Here's my answer," she called back to him.[9]

When Alice found out, she seized the opportunity. She invited Nick to accompany her on a junket to the Far East, planned for the long congressional summer break. Officially billed as an inspection tour of the Philippines, the couple would be chaperoned by Secretary of War and Mrs. William Howard Taft and accompanied by 600 congressmen, wives, and servants. Her parents, relieved that the trip would get Alice out of the newspapers for a time, readily gave their permission.

Nick agreed. Alice packed three steamer trunks, two hatboxes, and a container for her sidesaddle. The entourage boarded a train bound for San Francisco, then a steamer for the ten-day crossing to Japan.

The press had a field day. On the train platform Alice set off firecrackers and shot her revolver at telephone poles. In San Francisco, ignoring her chaperones, she slipped away and headed for Chinatown, then notorious for its opium dens.

In each country she was treated like royalty. In Japan, the emperor fawned over her and tried to install her in his palace. In the Philippines, the sultan proposed marriage offering to make her sultana of the Sulu archipelago. In China, she spent the night in the Summer Palace before her presentation at court. For that honor she was seated on a cushioned chair and carried in on the shoulders of eight men.

Although Alice came home with little information about the social and political problems of the countries she visited, she did bring back twenty-seven boxes of treasures.

Alice Roosevelt Longworth

By the time she and the hoard of gifts arrived back in Washington, Nick and Alice had decided to marry. All that remained was to ask for their parents' blessing and prepare for the wedding of the century. Although hers would not be the first White House wedding -- Andrew Jackson's niece, Grant's daughter and President Cleveland had preceded her in being married there -- hers would be the most spectacular.

* * * * *

When Edith put down her toothbrush on that day in 1905, she agreed that Nick and Alice should be married. Roosevelt came to the same decision. With their consent, and that of the Longworth's, the date for Alice's "Wedding of the Century" was set for February 17, 1906.

The bride-to-be barely had time to count the gifts from her Far East trip when the wedding gifts began pouring into the White House. Britain's King Edward VII and the German kaiser sent miniatures of themselves encrusted with diamonds, one on a gold snuff box, the other on a bracelet. From Pope Pius X came a mosaic of Vatican paintings, from the French government a Gobelin tapestry, from the Italian government a mosaic table and from the Cuban government a string of pearls valued at $25,000. The Dowager Empress of China gifted Alice with eight rolls of brocade, white fox and white ermine coats, plus a chest of white jade.

The couple also received hundreds of other gifts of sterling silver, crystal, and china from congressmen, justices, cabinet secretaries. No bride up to that time had ever received as many gifts. Piles of unopened packages remained in the store room for decades. Years later Alice said that the only thing she had relished about her wedding were the presents.[10]

On the wedding day, Alice arose at 11:00 a.m. with barely enough time to throw on her wedding dress. By 12:00 noon, thousands of onlookers packed the White House grounds as 145 carriages deposited invited guests at the east entrance. Almost 700 people crowded into the state rooms for the most expensive wedding ever held in the mansion.

Flowers decked the walls and windows of the East, Green and Blue Rooms. Every niche bloomed with vases of Easter lilies, roses, and pink carnations and asparagus fern. Palms lined window recesses. Great ropes of lilies and fern decorated every window and a forest of palms filled window recesses.

As the Marine Band played "Lohengrin", Nick's eight ushers escorted the president and Alice from the elevator. Father and daughter entered the East Room.

Alice wore a magnificent gown made from twenty-six yards of cream satin with an eighteen-foot-long train. Orange blossoms decorated her veil and around her neck she wore the wedding gift from Nick, a diamond necklace. From her bouquet, orchids cascaded. Since she had no bridesmaids they did not compete for attention.

The bride and her father walked to a platform covered with a rich Oriental rug where an altar upholstered in white overflowed with roses and lilies. There Nick waited, dressed in a Prince Albert frock coat with pearl gray cravat and gloves. The president placed Alice's hand in Nick's and the ceremony, officiated by the bishop of Washington Cathedral, began.

Following the vows, guests gathered in the state dining room. Separating from the larger group and their parents, Alice and Nick joined their friends to celebrate privately in the family dining room. When it came time to cut the wedding cake, Alice used the sword of a military aide to do the job.

At three o'clock Alice and Nick left under a hail of rice traveling by electric brougham to the McLean estate in Washington. They would take two honeymoons. After two days at her friend Evalyn McLean's sumptuous Georgetown estate, the newlyweds continued by private railroad car to Miami. From there they voyaged to Havana where they spent two weeks touring the scenes of her father's Rough Rider triumphs.

Four months later the newlyweds set out again, this time for a two-month trip to Europe. At each stop they were entertained at brilliant dinner parties, including those hosted by the king of England, the German kaiser, and the French president.

Returning to Washington, the Longworths took a house at 18th & I Streets. Here they entertained often, with Nick, a talented musician, playing his violin. Alice failed to appreciate Nick's musical talent, but she did enthusiastically encourage his political career.

She worked on Nick's campaign, though she was drawn more to her father's. Using the information and opinions she gathered while listening to congressional debates, Alice began discussing politics with her father's guests when she visited the White House. Her interest in national affairs grew. Soon, the once hedonistic young woman became one of her father's most valued sources of information and advice.[11] Using her contacts and her charm, Alice turned herself into one of the president's best lobbyists.

Although Alice and Nick grew apart (due to his womanizing and drinking), Nick's political career flourished. He won re-election as an Ohio representative for four terms and from 1925 to 1931 served as speaker of the House. He was so popular with the Republican party that it named the first House office building after him. With their new status, the Longworths moved to a palatial four-story house near Dupont Circle which Alice furnished with the finest antiques.

Two years later, Nick and Alice became parents with the birth of their daughter Paulina. But the attention he lavished on the child came to an end six years later with his death.

With Nick's passing Alice's dream of returning to the White House as first lady also died. Although she had influenced politics as the wife of a congressman and speaker of the House, what could she do as a widow? One answer came a year later when Ohio voters urged her to run for her deceased husband's seat. She turned that option down -- and a second bid a year later to run for the Senate.

Although she would not express her political opinions through office, she determined to do so by lobbying. When her fifth cousin, Franklin Delano Roosevelt announced his candidacy on the Democratic ticket in 1932, she declared herself a Republican and worked for his defeat. Alice had always disliked Franklin and his wife Eleanor, her first cousin.

When Franklin won the election, she refused the VIP seats reserved for her at the inauguration and instead listened to the event on radio at home. "When I think of Franklin and Eleanor in the White House, I could grind my teeth to powder and blow them out my nose," she snarled.[12]

With Roosevelt in office, Alice lobbied against the liberal administration, supporting instead conservative causes. Each morning after checking the newspaper to see which debates were scheduled, she would go to the Capitol, climb to the visitor's gallery and listen. At the breaks, she'd buttonhole senators and try to get them to see things her way.

To give her opinions and prejudices wider circulation -- and to ease her financial woes with remuneration through royalties -- she agreed to write her memoirs. Upon publication, her book *Crowded Hours* received glowing reviews and sales soared. With this first literary victory, she agreed to write a syndicated newspaper column, "Capital Comment".

Since Eleanor Roosevelt was also writing a syndicated column, "My Day", Alice decided to compete with her first cousin to see who could sign up the most newspapers. Alice won with 150 papers, twice the number Eleanor had.

The Democratic Convention of 1936 gave Alice another opportunity to attack the Democratic administration. Reporting for the *New York Herald Tribune*, she wrote of the "lethargical (sic) reception of the platform .... There is nothing in it to arouse fervor, even among the most susceptible of partisans."[13]
3

Four years later, Alice returned to the Democratic convention, this time to watch in "horror" as Franklin accepted the draft for a third term. Although Franklin and Eleanor invited Alice to the White House, their antagonist continued to attack them. Finally, disgusted with Alice, Franklin said: "I never want to see that woman again."[14]

In the same year that Franklin won re-elected for a fourth term, Alice's daughter Paulina married Alexander McCormick Sturm. But after only seven years of marriage, Alexander died, leaving behind his and Paulina's five-year-old daughter, Joanna. Paulina, devastated by her husband's death, moved into a house Alice rented for her and Joanna in Georgetown.

Six years later, Paulina, "an alcoholic suffering from extreme amounts of depression" died of an overdose.[15] At age seventy-three, Alice determined to take on the responsibility of caring for her grandchild. Bucking the opposition from her in-laws, the grandmother got her way. Joanna moved into Alice's town house, where she lived until Alice's death twenty years later.

In her last twenty years, Alice became "the most powerful woman in Washington's permanent social and political structure."[16] With her propensity for zeroing in on the truth behind the euphemism, Alice became one of Washington's most quoted sages. Her wit, style and indomitable spirit propelled Alice into society's inner circle. Influential people vied for invitations to her town house each afternoon where she served tea.

Over her lifetime, Alice knew a dozen presidents, from Benjamin Harrison to Gerald Ford. In her later years, she became good friends with presidents Kennedy, Johnson, Nixon, and Ford. The Kennedy's invited her to almost every state and private party. President and Mrs. Johnson invited Alice to attend the White House wedding of their daughter Luci to Pat Nugent. The Nixons invited her to their first dinner party of only ten selected guests. When the Queen of England visited the United States in 1976, Alice was among those invited to the state dinner by the Fords.

By the time she reached ninety-three years of age, all of the presidents, senators and speakers Alice had known were gone. "Most of my old tribal friends are either dead or barely tottering over the Hindu Kush on a Smithsonian tour", she commented.[17]

"All I've really done is to have a good time", she summed up in speaking about her life. A few months before her death she was asked how she felt about it: "I'm not afraid of death," Alice replied, "I'll consider it just another special occasion."[18]

***

Alice Roosevelt Longworth's Washington

Longworth Residence, 2009 Massachusetts Avenue N.W. where Alice lived for over fifty years. It's rumored she planted poison ivy to keep those waiting for the bus stop at her door from sitting on her stairs.

White House. Alice was married in the East Room.

Roosevelt Island, George Washington Parkway near Rosslyn, Virginia. With President Johnson Alice unveiled the statue of her father at his memorial site in 1967.

Longworth House Office Building, Independence Avenue & South Capitol Street, S.W., was named after Nick who was speaker of the House.

More Capital Tales

Like the glint of gold that catches the prospector's eye, so the hint of stories yet to be told entices the storyteller. Among the treasure only glimpsed on this writer's journey, these await the storyteller's elaboration and polish.

*B*aron Alexander de Bodisco, 1786-1854, Imperial Russian envoy. On the first Christmas after Bodisco's arrival in Georgetown in 1837, the fifty-two-year-old bachelor gave a grand party to introduce his two nephews to Washington society. Among the children attending, one captured his heart: sixteen-year-old Harriett Beall Williams. The first sign that Bodisco had fallen in love with the young girl escaped those who saw him walking to school with her each morning, carrying her books. It wasn't until he asked her to marry him -- and she accepted -- that people gasped.

They were married at the bride's home. She reigned like a Russian princess in a satin and silver lace gown from Paris with her golden hair enhanced by a crown of rarest pearls. He wore his splendid court dress of velvet and lace. To avoid the dilemma of naming one best man, Bodisco selected seven best men so that each of the bridesmaids would have a distinguished public figure as partner.

After the ceremony, the couple went by gilded coach to the Bodesco residence, 3322 O Street N.W., where a magnificent banquet awaited guests. Celebrations continued with an evening reception, morning-after the wedding breakfast, and a grand ball the next week.

By all reports, the marriage was a happy one. Harriet bore seven sons. Shortly before his death, Bodisco told his wife that after his death he hoped she would remarry and make another man as happy as she had made him. Six years after he died in 1854, the wealthy widow followed Bodisco's urging: she married an English captain -- a man very much younger than herself.

***

*C*onstantino Brumidi, 1805-1880, painter. Born in Rome, Brumidi's talent as a painter was nurtured from an early age. As a young man, Pope Pius IX commissioned him and three other artists to restore the Raphael frescoes in the Loggia of the Vatican. Also, Brumidi was asked to paint the pope's portrait. Because of that work, he was made a captain of the papal guard. But Brumidi turned against the pope during the 1848 rebellion by refusing to fire his guns at the insurgents. He was arrested and imprisoned. Fourteen months later, the pope released Brumidi telling him to leave Italy forever.

Brumidi emigrated to America and while getting his naturalization papers in Washington conceived of the idea of embellishing the U.S. Capitol. Hired for the job, he spent over thirty years decorating committee rooms, corridors and the great rotunda. After painting the fresco in the eye of the dome, Brumidi went on to paint with the frieze ringing the base. At age seventy, he began his work from a painting chair that was hoisted up the scaffolding to reach the surface that soars 100 feet above the floor. Brumidi was three years into execution of the frieze when his painting chair tipped over and left him dangling from the rung of a ladder sixty feet above the ground. Although rescued, he died shortly after.

***

More Tales

George C. Cassiday, Prohibition (1920-33) bootlegger to Congress. Born to a mother who held membership in the Women's Christian Temperance Union, Cassiday had never tasted more than a sip of brandy up to the time he went to work on Capitol Hill. Returning with an injury from service in World War I, Cassiday was turned down for the railroad job he'd held before the war because of his disability. He was looking for a job to support himself and his wife when he met two congressmen who introduced him to his life's work.

Restricted in their drinking by the laws of Prohibition, they asked if Cassiday could get them some good liquor. He complied and shortly after a member of the House suggested he move his operation inside the Captiol where he could use a vacant office.

Soon Cassiday was making twenty to twenty-five deliveries a day and running an exclusive drinking club in the House. Understanding the importance of constituents, Cassiday would take a few minutes away from his business to take important visitors on tours of the Capitol and pour them an illegal drink or two. "Some of them got a real thrill out of having a drink under the shadow of the Capitol Dome," he wrote in his memoirs published in the *New York Evening World*.

With a tip-off from several anti-vice congressmen, Cassiday was arrested in 1925 after five years of spirited service. Since he was wearing a green felt hat at the time, the sergeant at arms described to newsmen the person taken into custody as the man in the green felt hat. The name stuck. When he was released from prison, "the man in the green felt hat" was officially barred from the House. As a result, Cassiday shifted his operation over to the Senate where he continued his work as unofficial bootlegger for another five years.

***

William Wilson Corcoran, 1798-1888, banker and philanthropist. Corcoran, who began his career at age nineteen as co-owner with his brother of a dry goods store in Georgetown, twenty-two years later co-founded the Corcoran & Riggs Bank, which evolved into the present day Riggs Bank.

When funds were needed by the United States government to finance the Mexican War, Corcoran's bank bought the government's $16 million in war bonds, and sold $5 million worth to London's most eminent banking houses. That sale caused the market price of the bonds to rise and as a result his bank made a profit of over $2 million. With that fortune, Corcoran retired to devote himself to philanthropy, including the founding of the Corcoran Gallery of Art.

Corcoran's residence at the corner of H Street and Connecticut Avenue N.W. served as the first repository for his art collection. After purchasing it, he hired New York architect James Renwick, Jr., to enlarged and turn it into a Renaissance-style mansion.

Later when his art collection had grown and large numbers of people wanted to see it, Corcoran commissioned Renwick to design an art gallery a block away. With the opening of the Corcoran Gallery of Art in 1872, (today the Renwick Gallery at Pennsylvania Avenue & 17th Street N.W.), Corcoran became the first to offer the public a view of art masterworks.

Twenty-five years later, when Corcoran's collection outgrew Renwick's building, the present-day Corcoran Gallery of Art was built at 17th Street between E Street and New York Avenue N.W.

***

Henry Clay Folger, 1857-1930, lawyer, capitalist, philanthropist. While attending Amherst College, the man who rose to be president of Standard Oil Company of New York discovered the writer who he revered as the first of poets -- William Shakespeare.

A few years later with an "an ardor and intelligence unmatched in the history of book collecting", he began buying his works. Making his purchases secretly so as not to alert the competition of other buyers, he amassed the finest collection of Shakespeariana in existence.

In 1928, Folger announced he would erect a library in Washington to hold his collection of over 70,000 volumes. 80 First Folio copies, and other treasures. The cornerstone of the library at 201 East Capital Street S.E. was laid in 1930, but Folger never stepped inside his library; he died two years before its completion.

***

Samuel **Perpont Langley**, 1824-1906, pioneer in heavier-than- air machines and third secretary of the Smithsonian Institution. When Langley catapulted the man-carrying airplane commissioned by the U.S. War Department from a Potomac River houseboat, the machine plunged into the water. On a second try, its wings collapsed. Although ridiculed by newspaper accounts, he said that the aerodrome itself or its engines had not failed. "It is at this moment a success".

***

Eleanor **(Cissy) Patterson**. 1881-1948, newspaper editor and publisher. The willful and spoiled socialite moved through life with little sense of purpose until at age forty-nine she found her true career. When, because of her family's involvement in the newspaper business, William Randolph Hearst tried her out as editor-publisher of the *Washington Herald*, she threw herself into the job.

With her sensational stories (she interviewed Al Capone), her campaigns (home rule in the District of Columbia) and colorful gossip, Patterson doubled circulation in six years. One year later, she purchased another newspaper and combined it with the original one into the *Washington Times-Herald*. In 1954, that paper was sold to the *Washington Post* with which it was merged.

***

Rembrandt **Peale**, 1778-1860, artist. The son of portrait artist Charles Wilson Peale, Rembrandt at age seventeen asked his father to request George Washington to sit for a portrait. As his father engaged the general in conversation, Rembrandt was free to concentrate on his work. As a result, the young artist captured an expressive likeness of Washington which, after the general's death, he used to create the famous "Porthole Portrait" that now reigns above the speaker's rostrum in the Old Senate Chamber. That painting, second only to the Washington Monument as a tribute to the first president, grew out of more than forty years of effort to translate onto canvas his veneration for the hero.

Following the sitting, Rembrandt tried to capture his remembered image in sixteen different portraits. After Washington's death, when people grieved that no portrait adequately conveyed his countenance and spirit, a desire to create the perfect likeness haunted Rembrandt. The artist wanted to create a portrait that went beyond the representational to instead capture the monumental qualities of the man.

In 1823, Peale decided to spend three months in a last attempt. Working continuously on the task, he painted dozens of portraits, but each night, dissatisfied with the results, he dipped his rag in turpentine and washed off his days work.

Finally, as the three month period was coming to an end, Rembrandt worked his imagination into a frenzy and painted as if Washington had just left him. The memory of Washington's face twenty-eight years before was fresh in his brain. After painting all day, he again began to erase his work. But this time Rembrandt stopped. "Although the portrait was still not the perfect Washington to equal m my insatiable desire, I felt that I could do no more."

When the public saw the painting of Washington with its calm and benevolent strength, they praised Peale. Lawrence Lewis, Washington's nephew, said that the Gilbert Stuart famous portrait was in comparison to Peale's painting, "But a feeble likeness of Uncle". Peale took the portrait on tour of the United States and later abroad. In 1832 Congress appropriated $2000 Washington to purchase Peale's "Porthole Portrait" of Washington and placed it where it hangs today.

***

Albert Pike, 1809-1891, poet, lawyer, soldier, mystic. Although accepted by Harvard University, Pike lacked the money for tuition, so he set out instead to educate himself. From New England he trekked hundreds of miles through hostile Indian territory to St. Louis, Santa Fe and finally Little Rock, Arkansas. In Little Rock, he took a job as a teacher and began writing poetry which brought him international acclaim. At age twenty-six he was admitted to the bar and soon became the most sought after lawyer in Arkansas.

When the Civil War broke out, Pike served as a brigadier general in the Confederate army, but after Union forces took Little Rock, he retreated into the Ozark Mountains to write. In 1868 Pike moved to Washington where he continued his practice, served as editor of *The Patriot*, and studied Freemasonry.

Of all the adventures that crowded his eighty-two year lifetime, none caused a greater stir among his friends than the day in 1859 when Pike attended his own wake. Due to a confusion in names, friends believed Pike had died when actually the dead man was Albert Pickett. Discovering this, Pike decided to surprise those attending his funeral. Hiding behind a curtain he waited until the eulogies were read, then stepped out before his astonished friends. Using his well-honed oratory skill, he then regaled his audience with the story of his adventures in Hell.

During his last years, Pike lived in an apartment inside Washington's old Scottish Rite Temple. Although he left written communication that his cremated ashes where to be spread around the Acacia trees outside the building, his request was ignored. When he died for real the second time, the Supreme Council buried him in Oak Hill Cemetery. In 1944, Pike's remains were transferred to a crypt in the new Temple, an imposing structure modeled after the Seventh Wonder of the World, the Mausoleum at Halicarnassus, at 2800 16th Street, N.W.

***

Woodrow Wilson 1856-1924, 28th president of the United States. For the last three years of his life, the ex-president resided in Washington at the Wilson House, 2340 S Street N.W. Although his mind was clear his physical condition prevented him from active work and making public appearance. On one of the few exceptions, he traveled to Arlington National Cemetery on Armistice Day, 1918, to dedicate the Tomb of the Unknown Soldiers.

When he returned to his home after the ceremony, he was greeted by a cheering crowd gathered at his door. He entered the side door and in moments appeared on the balcony overlooking the street. The tired leader, who had failed to influence opinion to his high aspirations for the League of Nations, stood one last time before his public as the throng chanted "To the greatest hero of them all!".

***

Illustration Credits

Pierre L'Enfant
  print of Sarah Dehart sillhouette, State Department

Dolly Madison
  Gilbert Stuart portrait, Library of Congress

Stephen Decatur
  Henry Meyer engraving, Library of Congress

Peggy Eaton
  Henry Inman portrait, Library of Congress

Emily & Mary Edmonson
  Illustration from Paynter book, Library of Congress

Daniel Webster
  engraving, Library of Congress

Mary Custis Lee
  D. Appleton & Co. engraving, Library of Congress

Belle Boyd
  portrait, Wiilliam L Clements Library, University of Michigan

Frederick Douglass
  A. H. Ritchie engraving, Library of Congress.

John Wilkes Booth
  Old Print Shop engraving, Library of Congress

Daniel Sickles
  J.C. Buttre engraving, Library of Congress

Clara Barton
  John Sartain engraving, Library of Congress

Henry Adams
  photograph, Massachusetts Historical Society

John Philip Sousa
  E. Gluckaring photograph, Library of Congress

Evalyn Walsh McLean
  photograph, Library of Congress

Alice Roosevelt
  photograph, Library of Congress

Bibliography and Notes

Pierre Charles L'Enfant

Bibliography

Caemmerher, H. Paul, *The Life of Pierre Charles L'Enfant*. New York: Da Capo Press, 1970

Columbia Historical Society Records, Vol. 2 Washington, D.C.: Columbia Historical Society, 1899.

Columbia Historical Society Records, Vol. 22. Washington, D.C.: Columbia Historical Society, 1919.

Kite, Elizabeth, *L'Enfant & Washington*. Baltimore, The Johns Hopkins Press, 1929.

Notes

1. Kite, p 83
2. Ibid, p 95
3. CHS, II, p 216
4. Ibid, p 32-7, L'Enfant's letter to Washington, June 22, 1791
5. Caemmerher, p 198
6. Kite, p 151
7. CHS, XXII, p 150, Jefferson's letter to L'Enfant, Feb. 26, 1792
8. Caemmerher, p 213, L'Enfant's letter to Washington, Feb. 26, 1792
9. Ibid, p 294
10. Ibid, p 295

Dolly Madison

Bibliography

Anthony, Katharine. *Dolly Madison*. New York: Doubleday & Co., 1949.

Arnet, Ethel Stephens. *Mrs. James Madison*. Greensboro, N.C.: Piedmont Press, 1972.

Clark, Allen C. *Life & Letters of Dolly Madison*. Washington, D.C.: Press of W.F. Roberts Co., 1914.

Gerson, Noel B. *The Velvet Glove: Life of Dolly Madison.* New York: Thomas Nelson Inc., 1979.

Hurd, Charles, *Washington Cavalcade*. New York: E.P. Dutton & Co., 1847

Ingersoll, Charles J., *Historical Sketch of the Second War Between U.S. & Great Britain*. Philadelphia: Lea & Blanchard, 1849

Lord, Walter, *The Dawn's Early Light*. New York: W.W. Norton & Co., 1971

Madison, Dolly, *Memoirs and Letters*, edited by grand niece. Cambridge, Mass.: Houghton Mifflin & Co., 1886

Notes

1. Dictionary of American Biographies
2. Anthony, p 407
3. Madison, letter to Lucy Todd, Aug. 24, 2824
4. Gerson, p 220
5. Madison, p 107
6 Lord, p 147
7. Madison, letter to Lucy Todd, Aug. 24, 2824
8. Ingersoll, p 206-7 or Barker
9. Madison, letter to Mrs. Latrobe Dec. 3, 1814
10. Ingersoll, p 186
11. Arnet, p 245
12. Ibid, p 232
13. Gerson, p 223
14. Ibid, p 223
15. Hurd

Stephen Decatur

Bibliography

Adams, J.Q. *The Memoirs ... Comprising Portions of Diary from 1795-1848*. New York: Books for Libraries Press, 1969.

Anthony, Irvin. *Decatur*. New York: Chas. Scribner's Sons, 1931.

Lewis, Charles Lee. *The Romantic Decatur*. Freeport, New York: Books for Librarians Press, 1937.

MacKenzie, Alexander. *Life of Steven Decatur*. Boston: Charles Little & J. Brown, 1846.

Stevens, William Oliver, *Washington*. New York: Dodd, Mead & Company, 1943.

Tayloe, Benjamin. *Our Neighbors On La Fayette Square Anecdotes and Reminiscences*, privately printed by his widow. Washington: 1872; reprinted from the library of the American Institute of Architects by the Junior League of Washington, 1982.

Notes

   1. Anthony, p 299 (quotes Hambleton Memorandum of March 22, 1820)
   2. Ibid, p 295
   3. Ibid, p 303
   4. Ibid, p 287
   5. MacKenzie, p 322
   6. Lewis, p 227
   7. Adams, Vol. 12
   8. Anonymous, *Richmond Inquirer*
   9. Memorial to the President and members of the Senate, Nov. 24, 1849
 10. Stevens, p 63
 11. Tayloe, p 20

Anne Royall

Bibliography

Adams, J.Q. *The Memoirs ... Comprising Portions of Diary from 1795-1848*. Freeport, N.Y.: Books for Libraries Press, 1969.

Columbia Historical Society Records, Vol. 23. Washington, D.C.: Columbia Historical Society, 1923.

James, Bessie Rowland. *Anne Royall's USA*. New York: Rutgers University Press, 1972.

Maxwell, Alice S. and Marion B. Dunlevy. *Virago! The Story of Anne Newport Royall*. North Carolina: McFarland & Co. Publishing, 1924

Porter, Sarah Harvey. *The Live & Times of Anne Royall*. Cedar Rapids, Iowa: Torch Press Book Shop, 1909.

Royall, Anne. *The Huntress*. Washington, D.C.: Mrs. Anne Royall 1836-54.

Royall, Anne. *Pennsylvania or Travels 11*. Washington D.C.:, Mrs. Anne Royall, 1829.

Royall, Anne. *The Black Book, Vol 1*. Washington D.C.: Mrs. Anne Royall, 1828.

White, L.D. *The Jacksonians*. New York: Macmillan Co., 1954.

Notes

1. Royall, *Pennsylvania*, Appendix 21
2. White, pp 215-50
3. Royall, *Pennsylvania*, Appendix 21
4. Maxwell, p 122
5. Ibid, p 144
6. Royall, *Pennsylvania*, Appendix 10, p 214
7. Maxwell, p 188
8. Porter, p 138
9. Royall, Appendix 20
10. *New York: Commercial Advertiser*, July 7, 1829
11. *Harrisburg Intelligencer*, Aug. 4, 1829
12. James, p 261
13. Ibid, p 259
14, Royall, *Black Book*, p 7-8
15. Maxwell, p 190
16 James, p 312
17. Adams, p 321
18. CHS, XXIII, p. 104, lecture by Allen C., Clark, Oct. 21, 1919
19. Royall, *Huntress*, Feb. 22, 1845

Peggy O'Neal Eaton

Bibliography

Colman, Edna. *75 Years of White House Gossip*. Garden City, New York: Doubleday Page & Co., 1926.

Columbia Historical Society Records, Vol. 44-45. Washington D.C., 1949.

Eaton, Peggy. *Autobiography*. New York: Arno Press, 1932.

Gerson, Noel. *That Eaton Woman*. New York: Barre Publishing Co., 1974.

Pollack, Quena. *Peggy Eaton*. New York: Minton, Balch & Co., 1931.

Notes

1. Gerson, p 5
2. CHS, IVI-IVV, p 30
3. Gerson, p 22
4. Ibid, p 34
5. Eaton, p 47
6. Pollack, p 100
7. Colman, p 162
8. Gerson, p 82
9. Eaton, p 86
10. Pollack, p 107
11. Gerson, p 96
12. Ibid, p 99
13. Pollack, p 111
14. Ibid, p 112
15. Ibid, p 107
16. Ibid, p 129
17. *Washington Evening Star*, Sept. 18, 1921, by J. Harry Shannon

Emily and Mary Edmondson

Bibliography

Drayton, Daniel. *Personal Memoir*. New York: Negro University Press, 1855.

Paynter, John H. *Fugitives of the Pearl*. Washington, D.C.: The Associated Publishing Inc., 1930.

Stowe, Harriet Beecher. *A Key to Uncle Tom's Cabin*. St Clair Shores, Michigan: Scholarly Press, 1970.

Notes

1. Stowe, p 57
2. Paynter, p 23

3. Drayton, p 21
4. Ibid, p 21
5. Ibid, p 27
6. Stowe, p 157
7. Paynter. p 59
8. Ibid, p 65
9. Ibid, p 15
10. Ibid, p 69
11. Ibid, p 86
12. Ibid, p 111
13. Ibid, p 186
14. Ibid, p 189
15. Ibid, p 198
16. Ibid, p 200

Daniel Webster

Bibliography

Barlett, Irving H. *Daniel Webster*. New York: W.W. Norton Co., 1978.

Dalzell, Robert F. Jr. *Daniel Webster*. Boston: Houghton Mifflin Co., 1973.

Lee, Douglas Bennet, Robert L. Meersman, Donn L. Murphy. *Stage for a Nation: The National Theater*. McLean, Va.: EPM Publications, 1981.

Lodge, Henry Cabot. *Daniel Webster*. New York: Houghton Mifflin Co., 1883.

Steinberg, Alfred. *Daniel Webster*. New York: G.P. Putnam's Sons, 1959.

Webster, Daniel. *The Writings & Speeches*. Boston: Little Brown & Co., 1903.

Notes

1. Lee, p 38
2. Webster, *Writings ...*, Vol I, p 285
3. Bartlett, p 150
4. Webster, *Writings ...* Vol 18, p 398
5. Ibid, Vol 1, p 248
6. Steinberg, p 83
7. Lodge, p 225

8. Dalzell p 225
9. Ibid, p 143
10. Dictionary of American Biographies
11. Dalzell, p 240
12. Barlett, p 167
13. Ibid, p 167
14. Ibid, p 295
15. Dalzell, p 239
16. Steinberg, p 128

Mary Custis Lee

Bibliography

Columbia Historical Society Records, Vol. 31-32. Washington, D.C.: Columbia Historical Society, 1930.

MacDonald, Rose, *Mrs. Robert E. Lee.* Pikesville, Md.: R. B. Poisal, 1939.

Nagel, Paul C., *The Lees of Virginia.* Boston: Oxford University Press, 1990

Nelligan, Murray H. *Arlington Cemetery.* Washington, D.C.: U.S. Dept. Interior, National Park Service, 1953

Peters, James Edward. *Arlington National Cemetery.* Kensington, Md.: Woodbine House, 1986

Weigley, Russell F. *Quartermaster General of the Union Army.* New York: Columbia University Press, 1959

Notes

1. Peters, p 18, quotes Lee's letter to his sister
2. MacDonald, p 147
3. Ibid, p 148
4. Ibid, p 149
5. Peters, p 23-4
6. Weigley, p 341
7. Peters, p 25
8. Nelligan, p 498
9. Peters, p 26

10. Ibid, p 22, quotes Robert's letter to Mary
11. *MacDonald,* p 295, quotes Mary's letter to her daughter Mildred
12. CHS, XXXI-XXXII, p. 186

Belle Boyd

Bibliography

Boyd, Belle. *Belle Boyd In Camp and Prison.* edited by Curtis Carroll Davis. London: Thomas Yoseloff Ltd, 1968.

Kane, Harriet. *Spies for the Blue and Gray.* New York: Hanover House, 1954.

Scarborough, Ruth. *Belle Boyd.* Georgia: Mercer University Press, 1983.

Notes

1. Boyd, p 180
2. Kane, p 129
3. Boyd, p 165
4. Ibid, p 167
5. Ibid, p 194
6. Ibid, p 194
7. Ibid, p 261
8. Ibid, p 36-7
9. Ibid, p 41

Frederick Douglass

Bibliography

Blight, David W. *Frederick Douglass'* Civil War. Baton Rouge, Louisiana: State University Press, 1989.

Douglass, Frederick. *Life & Times of Frederick Douglass.* New York: MacMillan Pub. Co., 1962.

Foner, Phillip Sheldon. *Frederick Douglass.* New York: International Publishing, 1964.

Graham, Sheryl. *There Was Once A Slave*. New York: Julian Ressner Inc., 1947.

McFeely, William S. *Frederick Douglass*. New York: Simon & Schuster, 1991.

Notes

1. Douglass, p 347
2. Graham, p 101
3. Foner, p 58
4. Blight, p 161
5. Douglass, p 349, letter to George Stearns
6. McFeely, p 229-30
7. Douglass, Rochester speech re Lincoln assassination
8. Douglass, oration delivered at unveiling of Eancipation Memorial, April 14, 1876.
9. Douglass, *The Lessons of the Hour* speech delivered January 1894.

Daniel Sickles

Bibliography

Brandt, Nat. *The Congressman Who Got Away With Murder*. New York: Syracuse Univ. Press, 1991.

Fontaine, Felix, G. *The Trial of Daniel E. Sickles*. reported by Fontaine. New York: R.M. de Witt, 1859.

Graham, John. *Opening Speech of John Graham to Jury ....* New York: W.A. Townsend, 1859.

Pinchon, Edgcumb. *Dan Sickles Hero of Gettsburg & Yankee King of Spain*. Garden City, N.Y.: Doubleday Doran & Co. Inc., 1945.

Swanberg, W.A. *Sickles The Incredible*. New York: Chas Scribner's Sons, 1956.

Trial of Hon. Daniel E. Sickles. Washington: Wentworth & Stanley, 1859.

Notes

1. Fontaine, p 46

2. Ibid, p 72
3. Ibid, p 42-43
4. Pinchon, p 111
5. Brandt, p 121 (an amalgam of the trial testimony of eleven witnesses)
6. New York Daily Tribune, March 1, 1859
7. Defense James Brady, official records of *The Trial of Daniel Sickles*
8. Opening Speech of John Graham, Esq to the Jury on the Party of the Defense on the Trial of Daniel E. Sickles, New York: Times, April 27, 1859 & Brandt p 173
9. Graham opening speech
10. Brandt, p 171
11. "Trial ...", p 60
12. *New York Times*, April 27, 1859
13. *New York Herald Tribune*, July 20, 1959
14. Swanberg, p 65
15. Ibid, p 225

John Wilkes Booth

Bibliography

Bishop, James. *The Day Lincoln Was Shot*. New York: Harper & Bros., 1955

Clarke, Asia Booth. *The Unlocked Book*. New York: Arno Press, 1977.

Kunhardt, Dorothy. *Twenty Days*. Washington, D.C.: Harper & Rack, 1965.

Oldroyd, Osborn Hamilton. *The Assassination of Abraham Lincoln*. Washington, D.C.: Heritage Books, 1901.

Roscoe, Theodore. *The Web of Conspiracy*. Englewood Cliffs, New Jersey: Prentiss Hall, 1959.

Ruggles, Eleanor. *Prince of Players: Edwin Booth*. New York: W.W. Norton & Co., 1953.

Trial of the Assassination & Conspiracy in Washington, D.C. May-June 1865

Notes

1. Clarke, p 166. Also, an 1871 newspaper article by Warwick tells the story of Booth sleeping in the Lincoln deathbed, but Booth scholar and author Michael W. Kauffman believes Warwick did not exist since he can find no record of the actor in playbills, theatrical reviews nor city directors. Kauffman offers the explanation that the testimony of Booths friend, actor John Mathews, at Booth's trial was later embellished to include the mention of Booth's deathbed nap.
2. Kunhardt, p 31
3. Bishop, p 75
4. Roscoe, p 95
5. Ruggles, p 179
6. Oldroyd, p 69
7. *Trial ...* testimony by Edward P. Doherty

Clara Barton

Bibliography

Hamilton, Leni. *Clara Barton*. New York: Chelsea House Publishers, 1988.

Nolan, Jeannette C. *The Story of Clara Barton*. New York: Julian Messner Inc., 1962.

Pryor, Elizabeth Brown. *Clara Barton: Professional Angel*. Philadelphia: University of Pennsylvania Press, 1987.

Williams, Blanche Colton. Clara Barton. New York: J.B. Lippincott Co., 1941.

Notes

1. Williams, p 228
2. Nolan, p 86
3. Williams, p 165
4. Ibid, p 236
5. Ibid, p 243
6. Pryor, p 193
7. Ibid, p 195
8. Williams, p 256
9. Ibid, p 266

10. Hamilton, p 99
11. Ibid, p 104
12. Williams, p 435

Henry Adams

Bibliography

Adams, Henry. *Selected Letters*, edited by Newton Arvin. New York: Farrar, Straus & Young Inc., 1951.

Adams, Henry. *Letters of Henry Adams, 1858-91*. Boston: Houghton Mifflin, 1930.

Adams, Henry. *Education of Henry Adams*. Boston: Houghton Mifflin, 1961.

Blackmur, R.P. *Henry Adams*. New York: Harcourt Brace Jovanovich, 1936.

Friedrigh, Otto. *Clover*. New York: Simon & Schuster, 1979.

Samuels, Ernest. *Henry Adams*. Cambridge: The Belknap Press of Harvard University, 1989.

Notes

1. Freidrigh, p 318
2. Ibid, p 320
3. Adams, *Letters*. p 89
4. Friedrigh, p 314
5. Adams, p 229
6. Ibid, p 318
7. Ibid, p 133
8. Samuels, p 125
9. Freidrigh, p 318
10. Ibid, p 194
11. Ibid, p 320
12. Ibid, p 338
13. Blackmur, p 340
14. Freidrigh, p 13
15. Adams, *Selected Letters* ..., p 14
16. Freidrich, p 15

17, Dictionary of American Biography
18. Adams, *Letters* ... p. 271

John Philip Sousa

Bibliography

Bierley, Paul E. *John Philip Sousa*. Englewood Cliffs, New Jersey: Prentice-Hall, 1973.

Dictionary of American Biography. New York: Charles Scribner's Sons, 1928-36.

Sousa, John Philip. *Marching Along*. Boston: Hale, Cushman & Flint, 1928.

Notes

1. Sousa, p 111
2. Ibid, p 6
3. Ibid, p 26
4. Ibid, p 25
5. Ibid, p 26
6. Ibid, p 26
7. Ibid, p 26
8. Ibid, p 27
9. Ibid, p 18, author quotes from his book *Pipetown Sandy* which is based on "my own recollection of the impression" of Washington's Grand Review celebrating the end of the Civil War.
10. Bierley, p 9
11. Ibid, p 10
12. Sousa, p 365

Evalyn Walsh McLean

Bibliography

McLean, Evalyn Walsh. *Father Struck It Rich*. Ouray, Colo.: Bear Creek Publishing, 1936.

Notes

1. McLean, p 38

2. *Washington Star*, Dec. 8, 1903
3. McLean, p 175
4. Ibid, p 176
5. Ibid, p 178
6. Ibid, p 179
7. Ibid, p 161

Alice Roosevelt Longworth

Bibliography

Cassini, Margarite. *Never A Dull Moment*. New York: Harper & Bros, 1956.

Felsenthal, Carol. *Alice Roosevelt Longworth*. New York: G.P. Putnam's Sons, 1988.

Longworth, Alice Roosevelt. *Crowded Hours: Reminiscences of Alice Roosevelt Longworth*. New York: Charles Scribner's Sons, 1933.

Morris, Sylvia. *Edith Kermit Roosevelt*. New York: McCann & Geoghegan, 1980.

Teague, Michael. *Mrs. L; Alice Roosevelt Longworth*. New York: Doubleday & Co., 1981.

Teichmann, Howard. *Alice: The Life of Alice Roosevelt*. New Jersey: Prentice-Hall Inc., New Jersey, 1979.

Notes

1. Longworth, p 108
2. Teague, p 129
3. Cassini, p 166
4. Index of Women of the World
5. Current Biography 1943
6. Teague, p 129
7. Cassini, p 166
8. Ibid, p 200
9. Ibid, p 270
10. Teague, p 128
11. Felsenthal, p 116
12. Newsweek, Jan. 4, 1936
13. *New York Herald Tribune*, June 26, 1936

14. *New York Times Magazine*, Aug. 6, 1967
15. Felsenthal, p 231
16. Ibid, p 116
17, Teague, p 199
18 Ibid, p 252

More Capital Tales

Notes

Except for Bodisco and Cassiday, you'll find more information and reading suggestions on each of these featured individuals in the Dictionary of American Biography.

Index

A

Adams, Charles 138-139, 180
Adams, Marion "Clover" 137-142, 144
Adams, Henry 136-145
Alexandria 53, 56, 75-76
American Institute of Architects 5
American Presbyterian Church 30
American Red Cross 125, 129-133, 135
Anti-Slavery Society 57, 58
Appia, Louis 126, 128, 129
Arlington National Cemetery 6, 8, 77-80, 113
Arlington House 6, 71-76,
Arlington Memorial Bridge 6
Army Medical Museum 111
Arthur, Pres. Chester 131-132
Atzerodt, George 116, 118-119, 122

B

Bainbridge, Commodore William 23-25
Baker, Lt. Lafayette 88
Baltimore, Md. 33, 51, 56
Bank of Maryland 12
Barker, Jacob 13
Barron, Commodore James 22-25
Barton, Clara 124-135
Battle of Bull Run 84
Beecher, Henry Ward 57
Bell, Daniel 53

Belle Boyd in Camp and Prison 91
Berrien, John 41
Black Book, The 32
Bladensburg, Md. 15, 22-23, 27
Blaine, James 131-132
Bloody Run Dueling Ground, Md. 21-23, 27
Bodisco, Alexander de 175
Booth, John Wilkes 114-123
Botanic Garden 6
Bowling Green, Md. 121-122
Boyd, Belle 82-93
Branch, John 41
British 12-13, 15
Brookeville 14
Bruin, Joseph 56-58
Bruin & Hill, Alex. 61
Brumidi, Constanatino 176
Bryant, William 120
Buchanan, Pres. James 45, 127
Burr, Aaron 11
Butterworth, Samuel 107

C

Calhoun, John 37, 41-43
Camp Bird Mine 157
Campbell, Rep. George Washington 23
Capitol, U.S. 3, 5-6, 13-14, 33, 35, 46, 69, 87, 176-177
Capitol Hill 30
Carlisle, James M. 108
Carow, Edith 166
Carroll, Daniel of Duddington 2, 4, 13

Carroll Prison 89
Cartier, Pierre 156
Cassiday, George 177
Cassini, Margarite 168
Cedar Hill 102-103
Chancellorsville Campaign 110
Chesapeake Bay 51
Christ Church Capitol Hill 153
Cincinnati Inquirer 157
City Hall 29, 35, 110
Clay, Sen. Henry 66-67
Cleveland, Grover 150
Cockburn, George 13-14
Confederate Intelligence Service 84
Congressional Cemetery 153
Corcoran, Willliam W. 178
Corcoran Gallery of Art 178
Connecticut 90
Cox, Col. Samuel 120
Coxe, Attorney Richard 31
Cranch, Judge Wm. 30-32
Crawford, Thomas 109
Cristina, Maria 43
Crowded Hours 171
Custis, George Washington 13, 72-74
Custis-Lee Mansion (see Arlington House)

D

Dartmouth College 63, 65
Davis, Jefferson 76, 88, 120
Davis, Peregrin 120
Decatur, Commodore Stephen 20-27
Declaration of Independence 51
Democracy 137, 140
Digges, Thomas 5
Douglass, Frederick 94-103
Douglass Residence 103

Drayton, Capt. Daniel 51, 53, 55

E

Eaton, Peggy 37-44
Eaton, Sen. John 37-44
Edmondson, Emily & Mary 47-61
Edmondson, Paul 57, 58
Edmondson, Samuel 50, 52-53
Education of Henry Adams 142
Elliot, Jesse 23-25
Ely, Dr. Ezra Stiles 30-31, 33, 41
Emancipation Memorial 103
"Emancipation Proclamation" 98-99, 101, 103
Embassy Row 156
Evarts, William 130

F

Fairfax County 75, 77
Federal Hall 3
Fifteenth Amendment 102
Fillmore, Pres. Millard 64
Five of Hearts 137, 140
Floyd, Gen. John 88
Folger, Henry Clay 178
Foote, Sen. Henry 50
Ford, Gerald 172
Ford's Theater 114, 116-117, 122-123
Forrest Hall 91
Fort Washington, Md. 53, 55, 60
Freedmen's Monument (see Emancipation Memorial)
Freedom Plaza, 8
Franklin House 39-40, 46
Freedom Plaza 8
Freemasonry 181
Friendship 159

201

Front Royal   85-87

G

Gardnier, Rep. Barent   23
Garfield, Pres. James   130-131
Garrett, Richard   121
Garrison, William Lloyd   58, 97
Geneva International Red Cross Conference   132
Geneva Treaty   126
Georgetown   13, 160, 170, 175, 178
Gettysburg   110
"Gettysburg Address"   68
Glen Echo   133
Graham, John   108-109
Grant, Ulysses S.   111, 117-118
Green Hill, Md.   5-6
Greyhound   90
"Grief" Statue   142
Grover's Theater   117

H

Hagner, Dr. Charles   138
Hambleton, Samuel   23
Hammond   91
Hardinge, Sam   90-91
Harper's Ferry   74, 75
Harris, Clara   118
Harrison, Benjamin   66
Hay, Clara   140
Hay, John   137, 140, 142
Hayes, Pres. Rutherford   126, 130
Hearst, Wm. Randolph   179
Herold, David   116, 118, 119-122
High, Nathaniel   92
Hope diamond   156, 160
Hubbell, Dr. Julian   133, 134

I

Ingham, Samuel   41
International Red Cross   125-126, 128-129, 131-133

J

Jackson, Pres. Andrew   37-38, 40-43, 46
Jackson Administration   29-32
Jackson, Gen. Thomas "Stonewall"   85-87
Jackson, Rachel   40-41
Jefferson, Thomas   3-4
Jennings, Paul   50, 53
Jett, Willie   121
Johnson, Andrew   91, 111, 118-119, 172
Jones, Thomas   120
Jonhstown Flood   133
Judson   54-55

K

Kennedy, Pres. John   172
Key, Philip Barton   106-110, 112
King, Clarence   140, 142
Kirkwood House   118

L

L'Enfant, Pierre Charles   1-9
L'Enfant Plaza   9
Lafayette, Marquis de   2
Lafayette Square, Wash.   16, 18, 21-23, 25-26, 50, 69, 104, 140-141
Langley, Samuel   179
Laphan   132
Lee, George Washington Custis   4-7, 71, 73, 78-79

Lee, Harry "Light Horse" 73
Lee, Mary Custis 70-81
Lee, Robert E. 71, 73, 74, 75, 76, 77
Library of Congress 34-35, 179
Lincoln, Pres. Abraham 68, 75, 91, 95-96, 101, 114, 116-119, 122
Lincoln Memorial 6
Lincoln, Robert 131
Lind, Jenny 64
Lloyd, Edward 96
London 90-91
Longworth, Alice Roosevelt 164-174
Longworth House Office Building 174
Longworth, Joanna 176
Longworth, Nicolas "Nick" 166-171
Longworth, Paulina 171-172

M

Madison, Dolly 10-19
Madison, James 11-16
Mall, The 5
Marine Band 147-149, 153
Martinsburg, W. Va. 82, 84-85, 87, 89
Massachusetts House of Representatives 65
McLean, Evalyn Walsh 154-163
McLean, Edward "Ned" 154, 157, 160
McMillan, Sen. James 5
Meigs, Montgomery 77-78
Metropolitan AME Church 102, 103
Mexican War 74
Miner, Myrtilla 58
Miner Teachers College 58
Monroe, James 16, 40

Monroe, Mrs. James 40
Monroe Doctrine 129
Montgomery, Walter 91
Montpelier, Va 16
Morse, Samuel 33
Mudd, Dr. Samuel 120, 122

N

National First Aid Society 133
National Museum of Health & Medicine 130
National Republican 45
National Theater 64
Navy Yard 14, 29, 35
Navy Yard Bridge 118
New Orleans 56
New York 3, 41, 44, 57,
Nixon, Richard 172
North Star 98

O

Oak Hill Cemetery 36, 47, 181
Octagon House 15, 19
Ohio 90
Old Capitol Prison 82
Old City Hall (see City Hall)
O'Neal, Peggy (see Eaton)
O'Neal, William 38-39
Ould, Robert 108
"Our American Cousin" 117, 119

P, Q

Paine, Louis 116, 118-119, 122
Patent Office 125, 127, 135
Patterson, Eleanor "Cissy" 179
Patuxent River 12
Peale, Rembrandt 180

Pennsylvania Avenue 52, 56
Perry, Commodore Matthew 25
Petersen House 119, 123
Philadelphia 3
Phillips, Rep. Philip 108
Pike, Albert 181
Pitts, Helen 102
Point Lookout 53
Polk, Pres. James 17
Pomeroy, Sen. Samuel 96
"Porthole Portrait" 180
Port Royal 120
Presbyterian Church 30

R

Rathbone, Maj. Henry 118-119, 123
Ravensworth, Virginia 75-76
Renwick, James 178
Republican Party 171
Richmond, Virginia 89
Riggs Bank 178
Rock Creek Cemetery 141, 144
Rogers, Henry 33-34
Rokeby 14
Rollins, William 120
Rollins, Bettie 121
Roosevelt, Alice (see Longworth)
Roosevelt, Eleanor 171-172
Roosevelt, Franklin 167, 171-172
Roosevelt, Theodore 166-167, 169
Ross, Gen. Robert 13
Royall, Anne 28-35
Russell, Rev. William T. 6

S

Saint-Gaudens, Augustus 5, 141, 144,

St. John's Church 107
St. John's Episcopal Church, 46
Sala, George 91
Salona, Virginia 13, 14
Scottish Rite Temple 181
Second Bank of the United States 30
"Seventh of March" Speech 66-68
Seward, William 118-119, 130
Shield, Gen. James 85
Sickles, Daniel 104-113
Sickles, Teresa 106, 108, 110, 112
Society of the Cincinnati 3
Smithsonian Institution 161, 179
Sousa, Antonio 149
Sousa Bridge 153
Sousa, John Philip 146-153
Sousa New Marine Band 150
Standard Oil Company of New York 178
Stanton, Edwin M. 89, 108
Star Hotel, Bowling Green 121
Stowe, Harriet Beecher 59
Stuart, Gilbert 12, 17
Sturm, Alexander 172
Supreme Court 78
Surratt, John 116
Surratt, Mary 116, 118
Surrattsville 118, 120
Swainston, John 91
Swan, Oswell 120

T

Taft, Pres. William Howard 7
Tayloe, Benjamin 15
Taylor, Pres. Zachary 66
Temporary Insanity Plea 104, 109
"The Compromise of 1850" 69

Thirteenth Amendment   101
Thurston, Judge   31
Timberlake, John   39, 46
Tims, Henry   32
Tomb of the Unknown Soldier
    182
Tyler, John   66

U

Union Station   6
U.S. Constitution   64-65, 98
U.S. Navy   22
University of District of Columbia
    58
Upper Marlboro, Md.   15

V

Valley Forge, Penn.   2
Van Buren, Martin   37, 41-43,
    66
Von Steuben, Baron,   2

W

Walsh, Thomas   156
War Department   82
War of 1812   11
Warwick, Charles   116
Washington Club   112
Washington, George   2-5, 71-
    75, 180
Washington Herald   179
Washington Monument   5, 6
Washington Post   179
Washington Star   154, 157
Washington Times   160
Webster, Daniel   62-69
Webster Statue   69
West Point   73-74
Whig Party   63, 66
White House   3, 6, 11, 16, 38,
    40, 42, 46, 95-96, 100, 117,
    150, 166-167, 169-172,
White House Wharf   51
Wiley's Tavern   14
Williams, Willian Orton   75, 175-
    176
Wilson, Pres. Woodrow   181
Winder, Gen. William Henry   12,
    14
Winston, Harry   160
Wood, Willian   88
World Columbian Exposition   5,
    151

X, Y, Z

Yohe, Mary   157, 159

Mail Order Form

Please send **Capital Tales** at $15 per copy (plus $2 per copy for shipping and handling).* I understand that I may return any book for a full refund -- for any reason, no questions asked.

Number of copies _____ .   Amount enlosed $_____ .

Make check to: Mercury Press

Mail order to: Mercury Press
                  PO Box 34933
                  Bethesda, Md. 20827-0933

Name: _____

Address: _____

City: _____   State: _____   Zip: _____

* Md residents add 5% sales tax